THE NEW ILLUSTRATED GUIDE TO

WEAPONS OF THE
ELITE
FORCES

SMITHMARK

THE NEW ILLUSTRATED GUIDE TO

WEAPONS OF THE
ELITE
FORCES

DAVID MILLER
& GERARD RIDEFORT

A Salamander Book

©Salamander Books Ltd. 1992

ISBN 0-8317-5057-X

This edition published in 1992 by SMITHMARK Publishers, Inc., 112 Madison Avenue, New York, NY 10016.

SMITHMARK Books are available for bulk purchase for sales promotion and premium use. For details write or telephone the Manager of Special Sales, SMITHMARK Publishers, Inc., 112 Madison Avenue, New York, NY 10016. (212) 532-6600.

All correspondence concerning the content of this volume should be addressed to Salamander Books Ltd., 129-137 York Way, London N7 9LG, United Kingdom.

Credits

Authors: David Miller is an ex-officer in the British Army who now writes as a full-time freelance author on subjects of a military and technical nature.

Gerard Ridefort has spent all his adult life in military service; a career which has included the command of special forces units in Europe and the Middle East.

Editor: Bob Munro

Designed by: Phil Gorton and Paul Johnson

Artworks: Terry Hadler and Geoff Denney

Filmset by The Old Mill

Color reproduction by Magnum Graphics Ltd and Scantrans Pte.

Printed in Hong Kong

Photographs: The publisher wishes to thank all the official government archives and individuals who have supplied pictures for this publication.

Contents

DURING Operation *Desert Storm*, the US Navy's elite SEAL teams undertook 270 combat missions. Combat swimmers explored the Iraqi coastal defenses, SEAL patrols infiltrated Basra and roved far behind the enemy lines. When the Allied ground offensive began, SEALs raided the Kuwaiti coast to convince the Iraqis that an amphibious invasion had begun. In all these daring operations, the SEALs sustained no casualties.

American and British special forces acquitted themselves well during the Gulf War. While TV coverage emphasized the success of "smart" weapons and the breathtaking firepower of modern aircraft, the special forces played a key role in the Allied victory. The SEALs' achieved their success thanks to prolonged and arduous training, excellent equipment, and a deserved run of good fortune.

For obvious security reasons, the elite military units have no desire to make their activities public. Both their

personnel and their equipment remain concealed from friend and foe alike. Even the relatives of the US Army Special Forces soldiers killed in Iraq known nothing of their activities. The weapons and equipment of special warfare units remain shrouded in secrecy. The British Special Air Service (SAS) and the US Special Forces forbid the publication of photographs of soldiers currently serving with them. The Special Boat Squadron (SBS) does release pictures — but only from 10 or 20 years ago. Their amphibious role demands very unusual equipment which is only shown to the public when it *and the equipment that replaced it in service* are both out of date.

Special forces have always employed weapons and equipment developed for their own purposes, and different to those of regular infantry battalions. The first special forces, in the modern sense, were the stormtroopers recruited by the German Army during World War I. Selected from the very best of

Left: Members of the French counter-terrorist group GIGN display a range of weapons needed for their mission.

Diver
1 Breathing apparatus **2** Parachute **3** Distress flare **4** Depth gauge **5** Compass **6** UZI SMG **7** Propulsion unit

Night marksman
8 Protective waistcoat **9** Odelf image intensifier **10** H&K MP5 silenced SMG **11** Laser spot projector

Gas equipment
12 Smith & Wesson 37mm grenade throwers **13** Hand-held CS grenades **14** Tear gas spray **15** Protective waistcoat **16** Gas mask

Parachutist
17 Helmet **18** Goggles **19** Back parachute **20** Front parachute **21** Altimeter **22** H&K short SMG **23** Torches **24** Reflective gaiters **25** Flying suit **26** Parachute boots

Marksman
27 Radio headset **28** FR-FI sniping rifle **29** Sopolem OB50 vision device **30** Laser sight

A Climbing ropes **B** Colt Trooper .357 Magnum with laser **C** Sopolem OB44 night sight **D** CS gas grenades **E** Hand-thrown CS grenades **F** Manurhin revolver with optical sight **G** Attack grenade **H** Ruggieri blinding greande **I** 5-litre portable CS gas dispensesr **J** Helmet with clear visor

manpower, they were specially trained and provided with automatic weapons, light mortars and flamethrowers. These elite soldiers could succeed where so many others had failed: storming through the enemy trench systems and penetrating behind the enemy lines. Their superior weapons and tactics made them extremely formidable opponents.

By World War II, the weapons and equipment of the stormtroops were in service with most armies' regular battalions. But special warfare units were soon developed, and they too acquired unusual weapons and kit unique to their various roles. In the North African desert, the British introduced the Long Range Desert Group (LRDG), and Lt. David Stirling founded the SAS. British special forces introduced new and deadly silenced weapons like the De Lisle carbine and Wellrod pistol. The famous Commando dagger was invented by Captains Sykes and Fairbairn.

The weapons and equipment used for special operations today includes the full range of infantry armament. They also include weapons and personal kit more commonly associated with law enforcement or hunting; plus satellite communications gear and unique items developed for specific missions. Perhaps the most famous special warfare equipment belongs to the

Below: US soldier checking on Soviet weapons captured on the island of Grenada by US forces in 1983. Such weapons are widely available to today's terrorists.

SAS: since the storming of the Iranian Embassy in May 1980, the sinister black combat suit and gas mask of the Counter Revolutionary Warfare (CRW) team has become synonymous with the operations of special forces.

Countries like the UK, which has no law enforcement agency capable of dealing with terrorists, have to rely on their armed forces instead. The SAS, re-formed after World War II to help tackle the terrorist campaign in Malaya, had spent the 1960s fighting guerrilla wars in the Middle East and Asia. But events like the massacre of the Israeli athletes in 1972 gave sudden prominence to hostage rescue and associated anti-terrorist actions. The SAS began testing weapons and equipment for its new task: Uzi and Ingram SMGs were tried before the

regiment settled on the German Heckler and Koch MP5. The SAS experimented with body armor, gas, "flash-bang" stun grenades, abseiling gear and all the kit that the public saw on live TV during the dramatic assault on the Iranian Embassy in May 1980.

CRW equipment ranges from the latest products of modern technology to the fruits of low cunning. The team that rescued the hostages from the Embassy learned the layout of the building, and monitored the movement of the terrorists using fiber optic tubes pushed through the wall. By contrast, some US hostage rescue teams have home-made "shot lock" cartridges for their shotguns. The lead shot is replaced by a slug of dental filling material: fired into a door lock, it will shatter the mechanism without injuring anyone on the other side. If a unit has to storm a building containing hostages, it does not want to start the operation by accidentally killing one who happens to be standing near the entry point.

In conventional warfare, special forces units can usually afford to tailor their equipment to the requirements of the mission. For long-range patrol operations, special forces soldiers often prefer short carbines like the CAR-15 or AKSU. These are handier and lighter than standard assault rifles — and are particularly effective when it comes to close-range engagements.

The adoption of 5.56mm rifles by most armies has led to the submachine gun (SMG) passing into reserve or out of military service altogether. However, special warfare units have retained the SMG both for counter-terrorist and conventional operations. The MP5 remains the favorite — used by the SAS, SBS, US Army Special Forces, US Navy SEALs and several other organizations. Latest variants include a "Navy" version which is particularly corrosion-resistant, and another chambered for the 10mm cartridge, developed for the Federal Bureau of Investigation.

Special forces are also well known for their interest in sniper rifles. From

Above: Small, lightweight and very "high-tech", this mini satellite receiver dish is a fine example of the sort of state-of-the-art technology used by Delta Force during Operation *Desert Storm*.

typical 7.62mm weapons to the monstrous .50in weapons adopted in the USA, these are the most accurate rifles in military service. Since a Barrett sniper rifle achieved a confirmed kill at 1,800m during the Gulf War, the deadly reach of the sniper has never been greater. Combined with the latest night vision aids, a well-trained sniper can pick off key personnel and destroy vital equipment at any time of day. Large-caliber sniper rifles are now used to engage such expensive and vulnerable targets as parked aircraft, radar or communications vehicles.

The pistol, like the SMG, is not regarded as a significant weapon by most military forces. However, special warfare units still value the handgun both as a back-up weapon and for certain specific types of operation. From undercover action against terrorists to hostage rescue missions, pistols remain important. They range from classic assassination weapons, like the Hi-Standard .22in pistols used in Vietnam, to 9mm pistols with magazine capacities of 18 to 20 rounds. The development of exciting new pistol cartridges such as the 10mm and .40in Smith & Wesson, offer special forces an unparalleled choice of ammunition.

US Special Operations Command has recently awarded Heckler and Koch a $1.4 million contract to develop a new .45in caliber pistol. A similar deal has been offered to Colt. Both companies are tasked with producing a semi-automatic handgun with a laser aiming device and a silencer. The rival weapons will begin testing at the Naval Weapons Support Center in August 1992. At stake is an anticipated order for some 8,000 weapons. This is the first time an army has ordered a specifically offensive handgun since the 1960s.

Naval special forces have their own particular requirements. During World War II, Italian frogmen inflicted some spectacular damage to Royal Navy warships in Mediterranean ports. British divers and mini-submarines sank several German and Japanese ships in return. Since then, the capabilities of diving equipment and submersibles has increased dramatically. The full details of SBS operations during the Falklands campaign are still classified, but it is known that the SBS landed patrols weeks ahead of the main invasion. They reconnoitered the beaches, reporting details of the Argentinian defenses and even set up a concealed observation post inside the wreck of an ex-whaling ship in Port Stanley harbor!

Modern closed-circuit diving systems enable combat swimmers to operate in enemy waters, without releasing a trail of air bubbles to the surface. Dry-diving suits allow them to work in Arctic seas and in areas known to be contaminated by chemical weapons.

The collapse of the Warsaw Pact has led to the West's armies making drastic cuts in their defense budgets. Yet the continued instability in eastern Europe and the Middle East, not to mention Asia and Africa, ensures a continuing need for military preparation. The US Special Operations Command is actually receiving an increased budget as other units — primarily armored units formerly based in Germany — are being disbanded. The ever-present terrorist threat, and the proven value of special warfare units in conventional combat, have produced a sustained interest in elite units.

Special forces units conceal many details of their weapons and equipment. Too much publicity could jeopardize future operations and put lives at risk. What follows here is the most detailed examination of specialist equipment that can be published today.

Below: Troopers of Germany's elite Border Police unit, GSG-9, training to rescue hostages held by terrorists in a building.

9mm Steyr GB

Origin: Austria. **Type:** Self-loading pistol. **Dimensions:** Length 8.5in (216mm); barrel length 5.35in (136mm). **Cartridge:** 9mm Parabellum. **Feed:** 18-round detachable box magazine. **Muzzle velocity:** 1,181-1,377ft/s (360-420m/s).

The Steyr GB is an innovative handgun that was favoured by US Army Special Forces during the 1980s. Its unusual action makes it particularly tolerant of poor quality ammunition — hence its popularity with units operating in remote areas with limited logistic support. Manufactured by the Austrian firm Steyr-Daimler-Puch, it was discontinued when it failed to win the Austrian Army's order for a new pistol. The loss of the order was no reflection on what is a fine design: it was unfortunate for Steyr that the Glock 17 appeared at the same time and promptly won the contract.

The GB employs a gas-delayed blowback system of operation. When fired, some of the propellant gas is bled off behind the barrel where it retards the rearward movement of the slide until chamber pressure has dropped to a safe level.

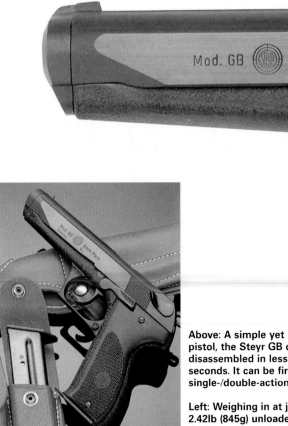

Above: A simple yet unusual pistol, the Steyr GB can be disassembled in less than six seconds. It can be fired in single-/double-action mode.

Left: Weighing in at just 2.42lb (845g) unloaded, this double-action automatic pistol carries an 18-round detachable magazine.

Most pistols using the conventional Colt-Browning locking system have difficulty with elderly ammunition; old — or badly assembled — cartridges tend to produce wide fluctuations in chamber pressure. Light loads fail to cycle the slide; heavy loads can damage the weapon. The GB's action simply bleeds off all the gas it needs to keep working: thus variable gas pressure is not a problem.

The GB introduced several features regarded as common in the 1990s but which raised a few eyebrows only a decade ago. Most obviously, the GB has no safety catch. Instead it has what is termed a de-cocking lever. If a soldier loads a magazine and racks back the slide, the pistol is cocked and the trigger needs a light pull of 4.8lb (2.2kg) to fire it. Whereas single-action pistols like the Browning High Power or Colt M1911 can now be made safe by flipping up the safety lever, the GB's de-cocking lever lowers the hammer. In this condition, the GB is still perfectly safe — it will not fire if dropped — but to shoot it, the soldier merely pulls the trigger. He does not have to disengage any safety lever. The first round requires a very positive 14lb (6.6kg) pull to fire — so an accidental discharge is most unlikely.

The 18-round magazine capacity of the GB also pointed the way ahead, and large-magazine capacity 9mm pistols are now in widespread service with the military and law enforcement agencies around the world.

9mm Glock 17

Origin: Austria. **Type:** Self-loading pistol. **Dimensions:** Length 8.97in (228mm); barrel length 4.48in (114mm). **Weights:** Gun without magazine 1.37lb (620g); with loaded magazine 1.97lb (890g). **Cartridge:** 9mm Parabellum. **Feed:** 17- or 19-round detachable box magazine. **Muzzle velocity:** 1,181ft/s (370m/s).

The Glock 17 beat the Steyr GB to win an Austrian Army contract and has now become one of the most successful pistols in recent history. Widely used by specialist military units, it is also fielded by over 40 per cent of US law enforcement agencies that use automatic pistols. In 1990 it was adopted by the UK's Metropolitan Police tactical firearms teams.

The same basic design has now been modified to fire 9mm Parabellum, .40in Smith & Wesson, 10mm and .45in ACP. All use the same operating system and are distinguished by high magazine capacities and light weight. Glock 17 pistols use a tough polymer material for the receiver; very durable, but much lighter than steel, it gave rise to allegations that the weapon was invisible to X-rays and so ideal for terrorists. This is nonsense since the slide, barrel and most internal

parts of the pistol are actually made of metal.

The Glock 17 has neither a safety catch nor a de-cocking lever. Instead it has what the manufacturers refer to as "Safe Action". The cartridge is fired by an internal striker. This is partially cocked when the slide returns to battery, but remains in a safe condition until the trigger is pulled. First, pressure on the twin trigger disengages the trigger safety; pulling further back fully cocks the striker, releases two more internal safety devices and fires the gun.

The Glock 17 is as simple to operate as a revolver: with no levers to fiddle with, it can be drawn and fired without delay. Unlike the Steyr GB and other pistols that are double-action/single-action, there is no difference in trigger pull between the first and subsequent rounds. This consistency is an important aid to accurate shooting. The Glock's trigger pull is adjustable — many military and law enforcement agencies have their Glocks modified to the "New York" trigger standard.

Glock pistols do not use standard rifling; instead of conventional lands and grooves, they employ a very efficient polygonal system that produces much more consistent muzzle velocities.

Below: The increased length of the Glock 17L Longslide can be seen in this illustration. Design is very simple throughout.

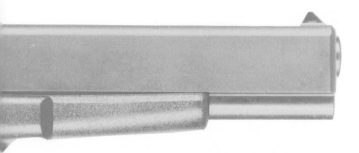

Below: One component from each of these Glock 17s was used to construct a gun which fired some 10,000 rounds without fault as part of a rigorous meltdown test.

5.45mm PSM

Origin: Soviet Union. **Type:** Semi-automatic pistol. **Dimensions:** Length 6.3in (160mm); barrel length 3.34in (85mm). **Weights:** 1.02lb (460g) empty, 1.1lb (500g) loaded. **Cartridge:** 5.45mm. **Feed:** 8-round detachable box magazine. **Muzzle velocity:** 1,033ft/s (315m/s).

The PSM was issued to the Soviet Army and internal security forces (both MVD and KGB) during the 1980s. It fires a unique 5.45mm cartridge and is small enough to fit in a trouser pocket. The Western interest in large-magazine capacity automatic pistols was never shared in the Soviet Union, and the PSM is the latest example of a very different approach to handgun design. To the Soviets, pistols have never been more than back-up weapons, only for emergency use. After World War II, most NATO countries adopted 9mm Parabellum as their standard

pistol and sub-machine gun cartridge; the Soviets opted for a less powerful round, namely the 9mm Makarov.

The PSM is little known outside the Soviet Union since it was never exported. Production ceased in the late 1980s after the Soviet forces had all they required. It is a slim, handy weapon, thin enough to be slipped into a jacket pocket without detection. In layout and overall design it is similar to the Walther PP, although the safety catch is further to the rear of the slide, further reducing the width.

The PSM's bottle-necked 5.45mm cartridge has a similar performance to the .22in long rifle round widely used in the West for target shooting and vermin control. It is accurate at combat ranges, and the steel core guarantees good penetration against body armor, but a 40-grain pistol bullet is hardly the last word in stopping power.

Below: The 5.45mm PSM strips rather like a Walther PPK. Note the cutaway magazine, typical of post-1945 Soviet pistols.

9mm Stechkin

Origin: Soviet Union. **Type:** Automatic pistol. **Dimensions:** Length 8.89in (226mm); length with stock 21in (541mm); barrel length 5.47in (139mm). **Weight:** 2.26lb (1.02kg) unloaded. **Cartridge:** 9mm x 18 Makarov. **Feed:** 20-round detachable box magazine. **Muzzle velocity:** 1,115ft/s (340m/s).

The Stechkin is a fully-automatic pistol that was issued to Soviet forces during the 1950s. Quite why the Red Army ordered the weapon has never been made public: some features of the weapon are distinctly old-fashioned, yet the final product is a very useful weapon for special forces. Issued with a wooden holster that doubles as a shoulder-stock, the Stechkin can be fired as a short-barrelled carbine and the sights go up to 218.6 yards (200m).

Most Western reference books deride the Stechkin as bulky, over-complicated and unnecessary. That it was only in production for the first half of the 1950s seems to lend credence to this view. The Stechkin was never exported to Warsaw Pact armies or client states in the Third World; only a handful have been examined in the West. However, the Stechkin is a fine weapon, superbly engineered with a blued finish equal to anything seen on commercially-made

guns in the USA. It is not heavy and fits comfortably in the hand. The light recoil of the 9mm Makarov cartridge is soaked up well and short bursts can be kept on a man-sized target at up to 27.33 yards (25m). The Stechkin was issued to specialist units including KGB and MVD detachments, and it is certainly still in use: a Bulgarian arrested for spying on NATO facilities in Holland during 1989 had a loaded Stechkin in the cab of his lorry. The KGB unit that stormed the Afghan Presidential Palace in 1979 made plentiful use of silenced Stechkins during the initial phase of the assault. The Stechkin silencer fits on without obstructing the sights and, combined with a collapsible wire stock, provides an assault team with a very compact automatic weapon.

The Stechkin has a rear drum sight which can be set for 27.33 yards (25m), 54.66 yards (50m), 109.33 yards (100m) and 218.66 yards (200m). Even with a shoulder-stock attached, this last distance is optimistic. The hammer-drop safety/fire selector can be set for single shots or fully-automatic fire and, at its cyclic rate of about 750 rounds per minute, a 20-round magazine lasts less than two seconds! The Stechkin's one weakness is its heel-latch magazine release which makes rapid re-loading impossible.

Below: Breakdown of the 9mm Stechkin automatic pistol, showing wooden holster/shoulder-stock, magazine and 9mm ammunition.

9mm SIG-Sauer P226

Origin: Germany. **Type:** Semi-automatic pistol. **Dimensions:** Length 7.7in (196mm); barrel 4.40in (112mm). **Weight:** 1.6lb (750g) empty. **Cartride:** 9mm Parabellum. **Feed:** 15-round detachable box magazine. **Muzzle velocity:** 1,099ft/s (335m/s) (115-grain 9mm JHP), 980.7ft/s (299m/s) (147-grain Federal Hydra-Shok).

Evolved from the German police pistol trials during the 1970s, this pistol was built for the US Army pistol competition that was ultimately won by the Beretta 92. However, the SIG P226 made a great impression and was described as "technically acceptable". Its combat performance was not the reason it failed to win the contract and it has now been adopted by many specialist military units including the British SAS. SIG pistols have a deserved reputation for quality and accuracy. They are also "re-assuringly expensive" which discourages some law

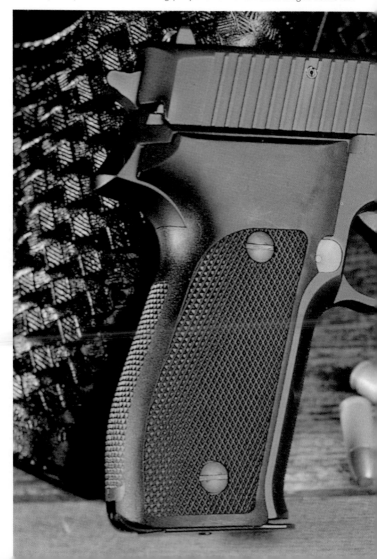

enforcement agencies and military organizations from acquiring them. Special forces, with more generous budgets, can afford to invest in whatever they like.

The SIG P226 has an aluminium receiver and formed sheet metal slide. It has no safety catch: instead, there is a frame-mounted lever that safely drops the cocked hammer. Once de-cocked, the pistol can be fired double-action, with a stiff trigger pull, or manually cocked for a more accurate shot. It has a Browning-style locking system: the barrel has a lug above the chamber that engages a recess by the ejection port to lock it to the slide. When the pistol is fired, a lug beneath the chamber strikes a crosspiece in the frame and lowers the rear of the barrel, disengaging it from the slide.

SIG pistols have become popular police weapons in the USA as well as Europe. The P220 is now available in .45in ACP as well as 9mm and a host of accessories are produced for SIG shooters.

Below: Robust and highly reliable, the German-built P226 has a 15-round detachable box magazine for 9mm Parabellum ammunition.

9mm Beretta 92F

Origin: Italy. **Type:** Semi-automatic pistol. **Dimensions:** Length 8.54in (217mm); barrel length 4.92in (125mm). **Weights:** 2.1lb (950g) unloaded. **Cartridge:** 9mm Parabellum. **Feed:** 15-round detachable box magazine. **Muzzle velocity:** 1,148ft/s (350m/s).

Now the standard service pistol of the US Army, Marine Corps and Air Force, the Beretta 92F is a stylish 9mm pistol that has sold well in Europe and South America. Its adoption by the US armed forces has been dogged by controversy despite the proven performance of the weapon elsewhere. With law suits flying thick and fast, and very lucrative contracts at stake, this unhappy saga seems set to continue for some time. One special forces unit is certainly not using the Beretta any more. The US Navy SEALs experienced more than their fair share of problems and abandoned the pistol after one sailor was injured when the slide fractured. The reported quip was *'you're not a SEAL 'til you've eaten Italian*

steel'. The SEALs used SIGs, H&Ks and even Colt M1911s during the Gulf War. Catastrophic slide failures also led the US Marine Corps to limit their Beretta 92Fs to a few thousand rounds only.

The mysterious cause of these problems has not been made public — it is deeply puzzling since identical weapons built by Taurus in Brazil do not appear to share the weakness. Other armies and even US law enforcement agencies have used Beretta 92s for years without any trouble. Sports shooters took to the Beretta without much delay — the lavish use of the Beretta in the movie *Lethal Weapon* providing a helpful boost in sales.

Comfortable in the hand and highly accurate, the Beretta 92F is certainly a fine handgun. It is the latest in a succession of pistols developed from the very successful Model 1951. Employing a Walther-type locking block, it has a double-action/single-action trigger and the obligatory large-magazine capacity.

Below: A 9mm Beretta 92F (right), successor to the Colt .45 Model 1911A1 (left) as the standard service pistol for US Army, Air Force and Marine Corps personnel.

9mm RAK PM-63 machine-pistol

Origin: Poland. **Type:** Machine-pistol. **Dimensions:** Length 13.1in (333mm) stock retracted, 22.95in (583mm) stock extended; barrel length 5.98in (152mm). **Weight:** 4lb (1.8kg) unloaded. **Cartridge:** 9mm Makarov. **Feed:** 25- or 40-round detachable box magazine. **Muzzle velocity:** 1,056ft/s (323m/s). **Cyclic rate of fire:** c.850rpm reduced to 600rpm by retarding device.

This was the principal weapon of the terrorists who took over Iran's London Embassy in 1980. Their fate in the subsequent gun battle with the SAS says more about the terrorists' poor training than their choice of hardware. Designed and manufactured in Poland, it is a handy sub-machine gun (SMG) that folds down small enough to be slipped under a jacket or inside a diplomatic bag. It is currrently used by the Polish anti-terrorist squad. The stock lies alongside the receiver when retracted and it has a fold-down foregrip. The standard 25-round magazine fits into the pistol grip and, like the Stechkin, is released by a catch underneath instead of a button mounted on the side. Once again, an Eastern bloc design team preferred to minimise the chance of accidentally dumping the magazine.

The PM-63 is built to a high standard for such a simple weapon. It fires from an open bolt and the slide must be racked back to cock it. The PM-63 can be fired like a large pistol. Indeed, it has one curious feature that could make it even more useful than most pistols: if you put the fore-end against a wall and push the weapon forward, you can cock it one-handed. As a back-up weapon for use when all else fails the PM-63 could be very useful.

Practical experience with the PM-63 soon shows why the users' manual only illustrates a two-handed hold. It is difficult to shoot accurately using only one hand because the bolt slams forward the moment you squeeze the trigger. This motion, and the change in the balance of the weapon, can only be overcome when the weapon is fired like a conventional SMG. There is no fire selector: a light pull on the trigger produces single shots; pulling it all the way back delivers automatic fire. There is a disconnector fitted to the trigger which, on a light pull, trips the sear and stops the slide until the trigger is pressed again. Pulling the trigger all the way back lowers the disconnector so that it is clear of the slide.

The PM-63's cyclic rate of fire is modified by a retarding device that restricts it to around 600 rounds per minute. This helps make it very controllable: firing short, aimed bursts from the shoulder, it is surprisingly accurate considering the sights are in constant motion.

Below: Sometimes referred to as the Wz-63, the 9mm RAK PM-63 is a compact weapon with a 25- (shown) or 40-round magazine.

Steyr AUG 9mm Para

Origin: Austria. **Type:** Sub-machine gun. **Dimensions:** Length overall 26.18in (665mm); barrel length 16.53in (420mm). **Weight:** 6.95lb (3.13kg) empty. **Rifling:** Six grooves, right-hand twist, one turn in 9.84in (250mm). **Cartridge:** 9mm Parabellum. **Feed:** 25- or 32-round detachable box. **Effective range:** 218.6yd (200m). **Muzzle velocity:** 1,312ft/s (400m/s). **Cyclic rate of fire:** 650-750rpm.

The Steyr AUG may look like a prop from a *Star Wars* movie, but it is one of the toughest and most reliable 5.56mm rifles in service today. The modular design of the AUG allows the same basic system to be everything from a shortened 5.56mm rifle to a heavy-barrel support weapon complete with bipod. The AUG 9mm is the latest version and the first in a different caliber. It uses the same stock and receiver as before but is fitted with a special bolt group, a magazine adapter, new magazine and new barrel.

The necessary components to convert an existing 5.56mm AUG to a 9mm sub-machine gun (SMG) are available from Steyr, or the weapon can be ordered in its complete form. The 9mm version is blowback-operated and fires from a closed bolt. Steyr has also developed a suppressed version for special operations: the only 9mm SMG to have an optical sight fitted as standard. In capable hands it will shoot five-round groups no larger than 4.9in (125mm) at 109.33yards (100m). The bullpup design gives a very good barrel length within a conveniently handy weapon: almost twice as long as that of the CAR-15, for example. The suppressor

Above: In addition to the 25- or 32-round magazine, the AUG A1 can fire rifle grenades such as these Belgian-built examples.

Below: Making full use of the x1.5 optical sights, Australian Army troops fire their AUG A1s. Note the ejected spent rounds.

supplied by Steyr eliminates the muzzle crack but, of course, it cannot disguise the sound made by the passage of a standard 9mm bullet. For completely silent operation, the user must fire subsonic (i.e. muzzle velocity less than 1,092ft/s (333m/s) ammunition.

Below: Ease of maintenance, operational reliability and much built-in versatility have made the Steyr AUG A1 a popular choice for today's armies. Ecuador's Ministerio de Defensa National was a customer for the Austrian SMG in 1987.

9mm Ingram MAC 10

Origin: USA. **Type:** Sub-machine gun. **Dimensions:** Length: (**Model 10**) 10.59in (269mm) stock retracted, 21.57in (548mm) stock extended; (**Model 11**) 9.76in (248mm) stock retracted, 18.11in (460mm) stock extended. Barrel length (**Model 10**) 5.74in (146mm), (**Model 11**) 5.07in (129mm). Suppressor (**Model 10**) 11.45in (291mm), (**Model 11**) 8.81in (224mm). **Cartridge:** (**Model 10**) .45 ACP or 9mm Parabellum, (**Model 11**) .380in ACP or 9mm Parabellum. **Muzzle velocity:** (**Model 10**) 918.4ft/s (280m/s) with .45in ACP, 1,181ft/s (360m/s) with 9mm Parabellum; (**Model 11**) 961ft/s (293m/s). **Cyclic rate of fire:** (**Model 10**) 1,150rpm with .45in ACP, 1,050rpm with 9mm Parabellum; (**Model 11**) 1,200rpm with either .380in ACP or 9mm Parabellum. N.B. *Cyclic rates vary depending on manufacture.*

This tiny sub-machine gun (SMG) is a brutally functional weapon which has enjoyed a chequered career in military service. Developed by Gordon B. Ingram, it first appeared in 1964 and was soon acquired by US Special Forces for use in Vietnam. Robust and very compact, the Model 10 fired .45in ACP or 9mm

Below: MAC 10 with shoulder-stock, suppressor to reduce the emergent gas velocity, 30-round magazine and .45 ACP ammunition.

Parabellum. With the stock extended and the long suppressor fitted, it was capable of passable accuracy when shooting single shots. However, the MAC 10's great claim to fame is that it has the highest cyclic rate of any SMG ever used by US forces. Firing at over 1,000 rounds per minute, a 30-round magazine disappears down range in 1.7 seconds or less.

The SAS adopted the MAC 10 when it organized the first Counter Revolutionary Warfare teams and began to practise hostage rescue. Like the US Special Forces, the British found the MAC 10 reliable enough and certainly handy, but its accuracy does not compare with the Heckler & Koch MP5. It is an excellent weapon for concealed carry and close quarter battle, but it lacks the precision demanded by the SAS's "killing house". The MAC 10's performance beyond point-blank range was so poor that in the USA it was dubbed the "phone booth gun" — because it had to be in the same booth as the target to guarantee a hit! The SAS soon switched to the MP5.

The MAC 10 was supplemented by the smaller Model 11 which fired 9mm Parabellum or 9mm Short (.380in ACP). As military and civilian sales waned, the Ingram went out of production for several years, but after several false starts it is now available again as the 'Cobray M11', manufactured in Atlanta, Georgia.

Blowback-operated, the MAC 10 has a cocking handle on top of the receiver with a 'U' notch cut through it to prevent it obstructing the sights. When the bolt is closed, it can be locked by rotating the cocking handle 90 degrees. One-handed shooting is possible but not particularly accurate on single-shot: fired on full auto it is positively uncontrollable.

Chambered for the .45 ACP and 9mm Parabellum, the Ingram MAC 10 is both short and compact — but accuracy is limited.

9mm Heckler & Koch MP5 sub-machine gun

Origin: Federal Republic of Germany. **Type:** Sub-machine gun. **Dimensions:** Barrel (**MP5A2**) 9in (225mm), (**MP5A3**) 9in (225mm), (**MP5SD1**) 6in (146mm), (**MP5SD2**) 6in (146mm), (**MP5SD3**) 6in (146mm), (**MP5K**) 5in (115mm); overall length (**MP5A2**) 26.8in (680mm), (**MP5A3**) 19.3in (490mm), (**MP5SD1**) 21.7in (550mm), (**MP5SD2**) 30.4in (780mm), (**MP5SD3**) 24in (610mm), (**MP5K**) 12.8in (325mm). **Weights:** (**MP5A2**) 5.6lb (2.5kg), (**MP5A3**) 6.3lb (2.9kg), (**MP5SD1**) 6.2lb (2.9kg), (**MP5SD2**) 6.8lb (3.1kg), (**MP5SD3**) 7.5lb (3.4kg), (**MP5K**) 4.4lb (2kg). **Caliber:** 9mm x 19 Parabellum. **Feed:** 15/30-round box magazine. **Muzzle velocity:** (**MP5A2**) 1,320ft/s (400m/s), (**MP5SD**) 935ft/s (285m/s), (**MP5S**) 230ft/s (375m/s). **Rate of fire:** (**MP5A2**) 800rpm, (**MP5A3**) 800rpm, (**MP5SD1**) 800rpm, (**MP5SD2**) 800rpm (**MP5SD3**) 800rpm, (**MP5K**) 900rpm. **Sights:** Rear, four operative rotating barrel; front, hooded blade, non-adjustable.

Below: One of the truly great weapons of the current era, the 9mm Heckler & Koch MP5 sub-machine gun, seen here in its A3 version, is used by many special forces around the world, including the SAS.

The H&K MP5 is the chosen weapon of most of the world's elite military units. In the USA it is carried by *Delta Force*, the FBI, the Secret Service and US Navy SEALs; in the UK it is used by the SAS and SBS; and in Germany it is issued to GSG-9. Each specialist unit has its own requirements and the close relationship between H&K and the Special Forces community has led to over 30 different versions of the MP5 being developed. The fixed butt can be swapped for retractable, folding or short stocks; trigger groups can be changed; screw-on or integral suppressors can be fitted — and in 1990 H&K announced a new variant of the MP5 chambered for 10mm instead of 9mm Parabellum.

The MP5 is a delayed blowback weapon and the bolt is locked at the moment of firing. Its superb accuracy makes it ideal for the sort of precise shooting required during hostage rescues. In capable hands it is as accurate as a rifle at up to 109.33yards (100m) — so SEAL teams are happy to carry it on operations against regular military forces. The basic mechanical design follows that of the G-3 rifle in which rearward movement of the bolt is delayed by rollers. The reliability of the MP5 has been proven time and again; like the G-3, the MP5 has a fluted chamber that lets propellant gas flow past the cartridge case. The MP5 spits out its empty brass with characteristic vigour, leaving distinctive marks on the spent cartridge cases.

The MP5 fires in one of three modes; semi-auto, full auto or three-, four-, or five-round burst — all of which are controlled by the trigger mechanism. Similar to the FN FAL, the H&K's safety acts as its fire selector.

One version of the MP5 widely used by specialist units and US police SWAT

teams is the MP5SD silenced version. The barrel has 30 holes in it to reduce velocity to subsonic levels and the integral silencer diverts the gas as it leaves the muzzle. Bursts of automatic fire are quieter than a .22in rifle and the extra weight of the silencer reduces muzzle climb.

When the first version of the MP5 appeared (adopted by the German police in 1966), it had a straight 15- or 30-round magazine. This proved unable to tolerate hollow-point or other specialist ammunition and was soon replaced by the curved magazine now issued as standard. The only exception is the new 10mm version

Below: 9mm H&K MP5 SD6 is a silenced version with a 30-round magazine, retracting butt-stock and a 3-round burst facility.

that has a straight polymer magazine that feeds all standard loads. The 10mm MP5 also overcomes the MP5's sole weakness — the lack of a hold-open device. On all other models the bolt remains forward after the last round is fired and the shooter can find himself squeezing the trigger on an empty gun.

Heckler & Koch was bought by Royal Ordnance in March 1990 but the change of ownership has not slowed the progress of this remarkable weapon. In 1992 there will be another MP5 model in production, this time chambered to take the .40in S&W cartridge.

Left: MP5 SD2 with a fixed butt-stock and a 15-round magazine. An optical sight can supplement the iron sights, as shown here.

Below: Special force soldier armed with an MP5A3 SMG with an optical sight, as well as a 9mm high-power Browning pistol.

9mm UZI/Mini-UZI Micro-UZI sub-machine gun

Origin: Israel. **Type:** Sub-machine gun. **Dimensions:** (**UZI**) 25.2in (640mm); (**Mini-UZI**) stock-folded 14.2in (360mm), stock extended 23.7in (600mm); **Micro-UZI** 10in (254mm). **Weight:** (**UZI**) 7.7lb (3.5kg); (**Mini-UZI**) 5.9lb (2.7kg). **Cartridge:** 9mm x 19 Parabellum (**UZI only**). **Feed:** (**UZI**) 25/32/40 box (9mm) or 16 box (0.45in); (**Mini-UZI**) 20/25/32 box (9mm only). **Rifling:** (9mm models) 4 groove r/h; (0.45in) 6 groove l/h. **Muzzle velocity:** (**UZI**) 1,312ft/s (400m/s); (**Mini-UZI**) 1,148ft/s (350m/s). **Effective range:** (**UZI**) 219yd (200m); (**Mini-UZI**) 164yd (150m). **Rate of fire:** (**UZI**) 600rpm; (**Mini-UZI**) 950rpm; (**Micro-UZI**) 1,200rpm.

One of the most widely used post-war sub-machine guns (SMG), the UZI was designed by Lieutenant Uziel Gal of the Israeli Army in 1949. The mechanism owes a considerable debt to the Czech Model 23 and 25 SMGs that appeared before World War II. The idea was to fit a respectably long barrel in a short weapon by adopting a different internal layout to previous SMGs. By wrapping the bolt around the chamber and putting the breech face back from the front of the bolt, Gal was able to get a 10.2in (260mm) barrel inside a gun only 17.5in (445mm) long. The magazine is in the grip which makes for the fastest possible re-load: hand

finds hand and in goes the magazine — much easier in the dark than trying to find the feed lips of something like a Sterling 9mm SMG.

The UZI operates by direct blowback using advanced primer ignition. It fires from an open bolt and is very reliable and easy to maintain. The cocking handle is on top of the receiver and has a slot cut through it so the foresight can be seen. A ratchet prevents it firing by accident if the user's hand slips off the handle just as the weapon is cocked. Additional security is provided by a grip safety which is released by the web of the hand when the UZI is properly held.

The UZI is used in the armed forces of Belgium, Germany, Iran, the Netherlands, Thailand, Venezuela and other countries.

The original UZI is now relegated to reserve status in the Israeli Army but newer versions are still in action with specialist units. The Mini-UZI is just that: a hand machine pistol only 14in (360mm) long with the stock folded; it is supplemented by the 9.8in (250mm) Micro-UZI.

Above: The Israeli 9mm UZI sub-machine gun is a blow-back weapon, in which the ammunition round is fired while the bolt is still travelling forward.

Above: 9mm Micro-UZI is the smallest, lightest version of the UZI family weighing just 4.7lb (2.14kg) fully loaded with 20 rounds. It is useful in maximum concealment situations.

5.45mm AKR

Origin: Soviet Union. **Type:** Sub-machine gun. **Caliber:** 5.45mm.
Ammunition: 5.45 x 39.5 Soviet. **Dimensions:** Length (extended stock)
26.6in (675mm); (folded stock) 16.5in (420mm). **Weight:** Not known.
Magazine: 30-round box type. **Muzzle velocity:** 2,625f/s (800m/s) (approx).
Effective range: 218yd (200m). **Rate of fire:** (cyclic) 800rpm (approx).

The Soviet Army used the 7.62mm PPSh-41 and PPS-43, fielded in 1941 and
1943 respectively, as its standard SMGs for many years. It then seemed to
allow the SMG as a type to die out, using AK-47 or AK-74 assault rifles where
other armies used SMGs. Recently, however, a totally new Soviet SMG has
appeared, which is clearly designed by Kalashnikov. The weapon is based
upon the AKS-74 assault rifle, but is much smaller and lighter.

The barrel is very short (200mm) and is fitted with a screw-on, cylindrical
attachment at the front of which is a bell-shaped flash hider. Unlike the great
majority of SMGs the AKR fires standard, full-charge rifle ammunition (in this

case, Soviet 5.45 x 39.5). In addition, due to the shortness of the barrel the gas is tapped-off very close to the chamber and these two combine to create very high pressures in such a small weapon. The muzzle attachment appears, therefore, to be an expansion chamber intended to reduce the pressure acting on the gas piston and also to act as a flame damper.

Basic iron sights are fitted. The rear sight is a simple, flip-over device, which is marked for 219yd (200m) and 438yd (400m). Despite the use of rifle ammunition the latter marking seems somewhat optimistic and a maximum effective range of 218yd (200m) seems a reasonable assumption.

The internal mechanism is identical to that of the AK-47, except that the gas piston, return spring and spring guide rod are shorter. The weapon also has a very simple skeleton stock, which folds forwards along the left-hand side.

The AKR will undoubtedly be used by Soviet and other Warsaw Pact special forces units. It will also presumably be exported to Third World countries and Soviet client states in due course.

Below: 5.45mm AKR, the latest Soviet SMG, is based on the AKS-74, but is much smaller. Length with stock folded to the left (inset) and locked into a spring-loaded lug on the receiver is 16.5in (420mm).

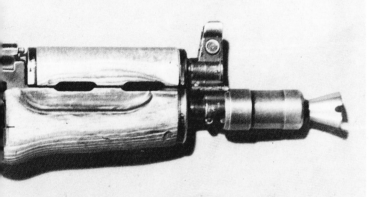

9mm L34A1 Sterling silenced sub-machine gun

Origin: United Kingdom. **Type:** Sub-machine gun. **Dimensions:** Stock extended 34.6in (864mm); stock folded 26.4in (660mm); barrel 7.9in (198mm). **Weights:** 8lb (3.6kg); loaded 9.5lb (4.3kg). **Caliber:** 9mm x 19 Parabellum. **Feed:** 34-round box magazine. **Rifling:** 6 grooves r/h. **Muzzle velocity:** Approximately 984f/s (300m/s). **Rate of fire:** (cyclic) 550rpm.

This is the silenced version of the L2A3, and is called the L34A1. It is somewhat longer than the L2A3 and tops the latter version's weight, unloaded, by almost two pounds (1kg). Many of its parts are interchangeable with those of the L2A3, thus keeping down replacement costs and ensuring weapon availability.

The barrel jacket is covered by a silencer casing, with front and rear supports. The barrel has 72 radial holes drilled through it, which permits propellant gas to escape, thus reducing the muzzle velocity of the bullet. The barrel has a metal wrap and diffuser tube; the extension tube goes beyond the silencer casing and barrel.

A spiral diffuser beyond the barrel is a series of discs, which has a hole through its center that allows passage of the round. Gas follows the round closely and is deflected back by the end cap; it mingles with the gases coming forward — with the result that the gas velocity leaving the weapon is low.

The silenced Sterling is used by the British Army, by many other countries, and terrorist groups. It is unusual among silenced SMGs in that it uses standard 9mm x 19 Parabellum rounds; other silent SMGs require special subsonic ammunition.

Right: British 'para' with an L34A1 fitted with a 10-round magazine. The L34A1 uses standard 9mm ammunition.

Below: Cutaway of the Sterling L34A1 shows radial holes in the barrel, the diffuser tube around the barrel and the spiral diffuser.

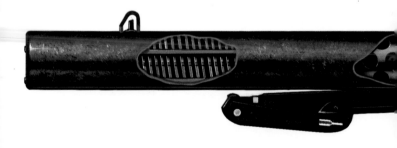

5.56mm FA MAS rifle

Origin: France. **Type:** Assault rifle. **Dimensions:** Without bayonet 30.28in (757mm); barrel 19.51in (488mm). **Weights:** Without magazine, sling or bipod 7.94lb (3.61kg); magazine, .33lb (0.15kg) empty; .99lb (0.45kg) loaded with 25 rounds; bipod, .374lb (0.17kg). **Cartridge:** 5.56mm x 45 NATO: M193. **Effective range:** 330yd (300m). **Muzzle velocity:** 3,168f/s (960m/s). **Rate of fire:** (cyclic) 900-1,000rpm.

The FA MAS (Fusil Automatique, Manufacture d'Armes de St. Etienne) is France's newest service rifle and has proven to be a highly effective and generally well-conceived piece of ordnance for general service and special

forces use. First introduced in 1973 (and subsequently modified), the rifle was placed into production in 1979. Delivery of the first complement of 148,000 rifles was completed in 1983.

Firing from the closed-bolt position, the method of operation is by means of delayed blow-back, the system having been adopted from the French AA52 general purpose machine gun. A black plastic lower handguard, pinned to the barrel and receiver, extends to the magazine well and cannot be removed.

Because it has a "bullpup" configuration, the trigger mechanism and pistol-grip have been mounted to the lower handguard, forward of the magazine well. The pistol-grip is ergonomically designed, with three finger grooves and a

Below: One of the most compact of the new generation of 5.56mm assault rifles, the MAS is now in wide-scale use with the French including special force units such as the Foreign Legion.

45

Colt Commando

Origin: USA. **Type:** Assault rifle/sub-machine gun. **Dimensions:** Length (butt extended) 31.5in (787mm), (butt telescoped) 28.4in (711mm); barrel 10.2in (254mm). **Weight:** (with sling and loaded) 7.1lb (3.23kg). **Cartridge:** 5.56mm x 45 NATO M193. **Feed:** 20- and 30-round box magazine. **Rifling:** 4 groove r/h. **Effective range:** 219yd (200m). **Muzzle velocity:** 3,049ft/s (924m/s). **Rate of fire:** (cyclic) 700-800rpm.

This shortened version of the M16 was tested in Vietnam as an alternative to a sub-machine gun (SMG). The idea was to deliver the accuracy and hitting power of an assault rifle in a weapon not much larger than a conventional 9mm SMG. The experimental version, designated XM-177, was used by US Special Forces, Rangers and by the Australian SAS. For soldiers moving through atrocious terrain, anything that reduces their burden is worthwhile.

A flash hider had to be mounted to reduce the excessive muzzle flash as burning propellant flared out from the cut-down barrel. Some Special Forces units removed this, feeling that the bright flash and incredible noise the weapon made were an advantage to a small patrol. In a sudden jungle firefight, a handful of men could sound like a much larger formation and make the Viet Cong hesitate long enough for the patrol to break contact.

'Most of the 52-man Special Forces team that mounted the abortive POW rescue attempt at Son Tay, North Vietnam, were equipped with XM-177s. They fitted Armalite Singlepoint night sights to them and carried extra 30-round magazines in canteen carriers.

The XM-177 was more often called the CAR-15. The production version was named the Commando and small numbers have been issued to various specialist formations in the USA, the Philippines and Central America. As a result, its use can be guaranteed for some time to come.

Right: 5.56mm Colt Commando is essentially a shortened version of the M16 for use by special forces in close-quarter battle.

Above: Colt Commando has a short barrel with considerable muzzle flash; hence the rather large, 4in (100mm) long flash hider.

5.45mm AK-74/AKS-74

Origin: Soviet Union. **Type:** Assault rifles. **Dimensions:** Length (**AK-74**) 37in (930mm); (**AKS-74**, with butt folded) 28in (690mm); barrel 16in (40mm). **Weight:** (unloaded) (**AK-74/AKS-74**) 7.9lb (3.6kg). **Rifling:** 4 grooves r/h; 1 turn in 7.8in (196mm). **Cartridge:** 5.45mm x 39.5. **Feed:** 30-round plastic box magazine. **Effective range:** 495yd (450m). **Muzzle velocity:** 2,970ft/s (900m/s). **Rate of fire:** (cyclic) 650rpm.

The current service rifle of the Soviet armed forces, the AK-74 is the latest version of the assault rifle invented by Mikhail Kalashnikov at the end of World War II. Operating in the same way as the AK-47, it fires a very effective steel-cored 5.45mm bullet that extracts the maximum terminal effect from such a light round. Like all Kalashnikovs, it is extremely reliable in any conditions; from the Arctic circle to the desert plains of Afghanistan, the AK-74 has proved itself a first class weapon.

The AK-74 can be distinguished from the AK-47 and AKM series by horizontal grooves in both the foregrip and the butt. The muzzle brake is very different, venting the propellant gas sideways in a superbly designed arrangement that makes it one of the most controllable rifles when firing fully-automatic.

Soviet *Spetsnaz* special forces pioneered the use of several AK-74 derivatives during the war in Afghanistan. The AKS-74U is a shortened model, with a folding stock, similar in concept to the Colt Commando. AK-74s were also used with an underbarrel 1.18in (30mm) grenade launcher, firing the same ammunition as the excellent AGS-17 belt-fed weapon issued to Soviet infantry companies. AK-74s were also manufactured in some of the former Warsaw Pact nations — the East Germans even producing one fitted with a scope.

Among the limitations of the rifle are that the gas cylinder is in a vulnerable position and, if dented, may cause weapon malfunction.

Above: Paratroopers of the Soviet Army armed with the AKS-74, a folding-stock version of the Kalashnikov AK-74 assault rifle.

Below: An illustration of the AK-74 with its folded stock. The cutaway areas reveal the ammunition and piston mechanisms.

5.56mm M16A1/A2

Origin: USA. **Type:** Assault rifle. **Dimensions:** Length overall 39.37in (1,000mm); barrel 20in (508mm). **Weight:** 7.55lb (3.4kg) empty, 8.55lb (3.85kg) with loaded 30-round magazine. **Caliber:** 5.56mm x 45 NATO SS109. **Feed:** 39-round box magazine. **Maximum effective range:** 437.2yard (400m). **Muzzle velocity:** 3,280ft/s (1,000m/s). **Cyclic rate of fire:** 600-940rpm.

The M16A2 is the standard service rifle of the US Army. It has been widely exported, and the civilian AR-15 Sporter is a popular target-shooting rifle in the US. The original AR-15 first saw action in Vietnam, when the US Air Force ordered 8,000 rifles for air base defence in 1962. The Army was impressed too and ordered 85,000 the following year. Designated the M16A1, it had a mixed reception thanks to a combination of poorly-trained troops and an unannounced change in the propellant used in US military ammunition. It is significant that few specialist units complained about the M16: on the contrary, they valued its light weight and accuracy.

The M16 is gas-operated, but its design does make it sensitive to propellant that leaves too much residue. Most gas-operated rifles divert the gas produced on firing into a gas cylinder; there, it drives back a piston which acts on the bolt and continues the firing cycle. On the M16 there is no gas cylinder: the gas produced on firing is piped directly backwards and works directly on the bolt carrier, blowing it to the rear.

The M16A2 was introduced in 1985 and incorporated a number of modifications made in the light of US experience in Vietnam. The M16A1's fully-automatic capability was replaced by a three-round burst facility. The US Army recognized that many soldiers in South-East Asia had tended to fire long bursts of automatic fire, and that after about three shots the muzzle climbed high enough to make the rest miss. In dry conditions, the M16A1's flash hider blew up dirt and debris because it had a hole in its underside: this has been removed on the M16A2.

The M16A2 is substantially lighter than most other 5.56mm military rifles. It is highly reliable and as accurate as can be, given the limitations of the SS109

Above: The longer barrel of the M16A2 (background) is visible when compared to that of the 5.56mm Colt Commando (foreground).

cartridge. Exhaustive tests by the US Army showed that state-of-the-art "advanced rifles" offered by the world's leading arms companies cannot offer a substantially better performance, and in 1990 the US Army announced that the M16 would continue in service for the foreseeable future. It will now be upgraded to M16A3 standard, which primarily involves the fitting of an optical sight. The M16 remains a popular weapon outside the US, particularly with speical forces. British SAS and SBS personnel used it in the Falklands War and during the 1991 Gulf War.

Below: Synonymous with the US Army soldier for some 30 years, the M16 will serve in the front-line for many years to come.

5.56mm & 7.62mm Galil assault rifle

Origin: Israel. **Type:** Assault rifle. **Dimensions:** Length, stock extended, 5.56 model 38.6in (979mm), 7.62 model 41.3in (1,050mm); stock folded, 5.56 model 29.2in (742mm), 7.62 model 31.9in (810mm). Barrel, 5.56 model 18.1in (460mm), 7.62 model 21 in (533mm). **Weight:** 5.56 model 8.6lb (3.9kg); 7.62 model 8.7lb (3.95kg). **Caliber:** 5.56mm or 7.62mm. **Max effective range:** 5.56 model 550yd (500m); 7.62 model 660yd (600m). **Muzzle velocity:** 5.56 model 3,230f/s (980m/s); 7.62 model 2,800f/s (850m/s). **Rate of fire:** Both models 650rpm.

Israel's Galil assault rifle, first issued in 1973, has a rich, battle-tested heritage. The system of the Galil is actually that of the Soviet AK-47 Kalashnikov, the most widely distributed and used of all assault rifles.

Credit for the rifle's development is given to an Israeli ordnance officer named Uziel Gal, along with Israel Military Industries. They realised that by using the full-scale Finnish Valmet M-60/62 receiver and a stout but not-too-heavy barrel, the system would serve both the 5.56 NATO cartridge and the 7.62 NATO round as well.

The operating system is a rotating bolt gas system and, with the exception of the stamped steel breech cover, the Galil is fully machined. The foregrip is wood, lined with Dural, and has ample clearance around the barrel for heat dissipation. When extended, the butt-stock has a positive latching system which prevents wobble by wedging the hinge end's tapered latching lugs into corresponding slots.

These are released by the simple expedient of squeezing with the right hand and folding the stock outward. The bipod folds and rotates into a slot on the underside of the foregrip, where the legs then spread apart by spring tension to latch into retaining slots.

The ambidextrous safety switch on the left side is a small lever, but its reciprocal right-side member also acts as an ejection port cover. The magazine is held by a catch in front of the trigger guard. To operate, the lever is taken off "safe" and the cocking handle pulled to the rear. When released, the carrier is driven forward and the top round is pushed from the magazine into the chamber.

The bolt comes to a halt and the cam pin (engaged in a slot in the carrier) rotates the bolt, which forces the cartridge forward, whereupon the extractor slips over the rim and the gun is ready to be fired.

Above: Israeli soldier with stock folded on his 5.56mm ARM assault rifle. The Galil has been thoroughly combat tested in many wars.

The system used for the trigger and firing mechanism is that employed in the M1 Garand rifle, the AK series and many others. Thirty-five rounds are held in the 5.56mm magazine and a 50-round magazine has also been produced. The 7.62mm magazine holds 25 rounds.

Sights for the Galil are folding "L" rear with two peeps, one for 330yd (300m), and a second for 550yd (500m). Unique to the system is its set of folding night sights which use tritium for illumination. For close quarter work at night or in a dark jungle, these sights are undetectable.

The Galil was adopted by South Africa after incorporating certain preferred modifications (such as carbon plastic stock instead of steel tubing to better fit terrain needs) and is called the R4 (Rifle 4). The R4 has proved itself in South West Africa and Angolan operations.

Below: Solid stock version of the very effective Galil 5.56mm automatic rifle, produced by Israel Military Industries (IMI).

Model PM/L96A1

Origin: UK. **Type:** Sniper rifle. **Caliber:** 7.62mm x 51, .300in Win. Mag,
7mm Remington Magnum or .338in Lapua Magnum (8.6mm x 70).
Dimensions: Length 45.78in (1,163mm), (**Super Magnum**) 45.98in
(1,168mm), (**suppressed model**) 47.24in (1,200mm); barrel length: 25.78in
(655mm), (**.338 Super Magnum**) 26.96in (685mm), (**.300 or 7mm Super
Magnum**) 25.98in (660mm). **Weight:** 13.77lb (6.20kg), (**Super Magnum**)
15.11lb (6.80kg). **Feed:** (**7.62mm models**), 10-round detachable box
magazine; (**.338 Super Magnum**), 4 rounds; (**.300 or 7mm Super
Magnum**), 5 rounds.

The L96A1 is the British Army's current sniper rifle, issued to Army and Royal
Marine snipers. Designed and manufactured by Accuracy International, it fulfils
the British forces' requirement for a guaranteed hit at 600 yards (549m) and the
ability to harass enemy units at up to 1,000 yards (915m). At a time when many
armies are adopting self-loading weapons for sniping, the British decision to
persevere with a bolt-action rifle may seem rather reactionary. There is no doubt
that a good self-loading rifle allows the shooter to get off a faster second shot,
if one is required. However, unlike some bolt-action weapons, the L96A1 has
a bolt that can be operated without the shooter having to move his head and
lose his sight picture.

The olive green stock of the L96A1 does not form a structural part of the system.
The stainless steel barrel is free-floating within the stock. On conventional
wooden-stocked rifles which have the barrel and stock secured together, the
point of impact can vary because the wood expands or contracts according to
temperature and humidity. The high-impact plastic stock of the L96A1 is
ampidextrous and can be adjusted to suit the operational requirements of
individual shooters.

Like most modern sniper rifles, the L96A1 has an integral bipod; and it can
also be fitted with a retractable spike under the butt. Many sniper operations
involve protracted observation of a target area; using the spike, the rifle can be
set on target and left there without the sniper having to remain in a firing position
all the time. The construction of the L96A1 is commendably straightforward and
the sniper can maintain it in all but the most major repairs. The rifle can be stripped
down in about five minutes using three Allen keys and a screwdriver. The barrel
can be changed in a similar time without having to strip the rest of the weapon.
The trigger, too, can be removed and adjusted without dismantling the entire
weapon.

Designated the Model PM by the manufacturer, the L96A1 is available in several

Above: An L96A1 fitted with a Simrad Optronics KN250 night sight atop a PM 2 — 10 x 56 telescopic sight.

different versions. There is a suppressed model which has an effective range of 328 yards (300m) using subsonic 7.62mm ammunition. This is also produced in a take-down format, called the "covert" sniper rifle system. The rifle can be dismantled so that it fits into a suitcase complete with wheels and retractable handle. Inside is the rifle, two magazines, a scope and 20 rounds of subsonic ammunition. There is also the "Super Magnum" version which fires .338in Lapua Magnum, .300in Winchester Magnum or 7mm Remington Magnum. All three calibers offer a significant range advantage over 7.62mm ammunition, the .338in round offering a convenient compromise between 7.62mm and .50in caliber. This 250-grain round shoots to a much flatter trajectory and has about half the wind drift of 7.62mm rounds.

Below: Of very simple construction, the L96A1 can be stripped with three allen keys and one screwdriver in five minutes.

Heckler & Koch PSG-1

Origin: Germany. **Type:** Sniper rifle. **Dimensions:** Length 47.55in (1,208mm); barrel 25.59in (650mm). **Weight:** 20.88lb (9.4kg) loaded with 20-round magazine and fitted with tripod. **Cartridge:** 7.62mm x 51 NATO; Lapua .308in Winchester Match ammunition recommended. **Feed:** 5- or 20-round detachable box magazine.

The German company of Heckler & Koch, acquired by Royal Ordnance in 1990, is a prolific supplier of weapons to special warfare units. The PSG-1 complements the H&K MP5 sub-machine gun and the P7 and P9 pistols also widely employed by elite units of the western world. The semi-automatic PSG-1 is based on the veteran G3 full-auto 7.62mm assault rifle, still in service with the German Army and widely exported.

Using the same roller-locking system as the G3, the PSG-1 has a heavy barrel with a polygonal bore. Instead of the lands and grooves of conventional barrels, the inner surface has four grooves that twist gently to the right. Freeze-frame photography of bullets leaving a muzzle shows that this type of rifling is more efficient, because very little of the propellant gas manages to bypass the bullet and exit first. With a conventionally-rifled weapon, some of the gas passes through the gaps between the grooves and the side of the bullet. The result is a slight loss of velocity, and constantly-varying muzzle velocity.

On a service rifle, this is not important; but to the sniper, who must iron out every inconsistency to achieve the best results, polygonal rifling is another useful advantage. It is worth noting that this is not a new idea — British Whitworth sniper rifles used in the American Civil War employed a similar mechanism. They too could manage to pick off enemy officers at upwards of 800 yards (732m).

Right above: The PSG-1 sniping rifle was developed for police and special forces. It uses the H&K roller-lock bolt system.

Right: Numerous adjustments are possible, including butt-stock length, pivoted butt cap and vertically movable cheek piece.

Below: Designed for the specialist and highly trained marksman, the PSG1 is one of the most effective sniper rifles available.

7.62mm Dragunov (SVD) sniper rifle

Origin: Soviet Union. **Type:** Sniper rifle. **Dimensions:** Length 48.22in (1,225mm); barrel 53.93in (1,370mm). **Weight:** 10.26lb (4.62kg) loaded with 10-round magazine and PSO-1 scope fitted. **Cartridge:** 7.62mm x 54R. **Muzzle velocity:** 2,722ft/s (830m/s).

Unlike the British and American forces, the Soviet Army has always believed in the value of sniping. Soviet snipers — some of them women — played a major role during World War II, several individual snipers being credited with over 100 confirmed kills. Since most sniper victims are key personnel — officers, NCOs or specialist weapons crew — the impact of these snipers was enormous.

The SVD is a semi-automatic rifle, firing the same cartridge as the Soviet service rifle of World War I. Every Soviet motor rifle platoon has a sniper armed with an SVD, so this is much more than a special forces rifle. Boys who excelled at shooting with the communist youth movement are often picked to become the unit sniper when they are conscripted.

With its skeleton stock and impressive length, the SVD is instantly recognizable. The fire selector is similar to that of the Kalashnikov assault rifles, and any soldier trained on an AK could take over an SVD in an emergency. Dedicated western sniper rifles like the British L96 or American M21 have nothing in common with the standard service rifle.

The SVD is fitted with a PSO-1 scope which has x4 magnification and an illuminated reticle. Built to take hard punishment in the field, this is an excellent military scope, designed to keep working in conditions where finer but more fragile kit will probably fail. It also has simple rangefinding stadia common to sights on Soviet tank and anti-tank guns.

Half the weight of monsters like the PSG-1, the SVD is comfortable and pleasant to shoot. The extended rubber eyepiece gives the shooter proper eye relief and a good sight picture. In reasonable conditions, it will hit a man-size target at up to 655.6 yards (600m) without difficulty, but its long-range capability is not quite as good as more recent designs such as the excellent Parker Hale M85. The SVD was used throughout the Warsaw Pact and continues in service with many eastern European forces. It is also manufactured in China for the Chinese Army. A sporting version is widely used for hunting in the Soviet Union.

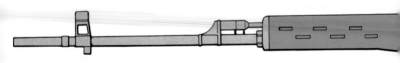

Above: The 7.62mm Dragunov (SVD) is now the standard sniper rifle for Soviet special forces; it is simple and very accurate.

Above: The SVD incorporates the lessons learned by the Soviets over many years of concentrated effort in military sniping.

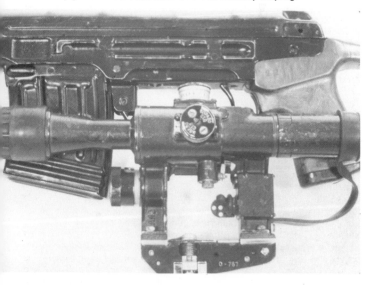

Above: The telescopic sight used on the SVD is a detachable, non-variable, x4 scope, with an extension tube to give eye relief.

7.62mm FR-F2

Origin: France. **Type:** Sniper rifle. **Length:** 47.24in (1,200mm); barrel length 25.59in (650mm). **Weight:** Wooden stock version with scope 11.86lb (5.34kg); composite stock model with scope 12.75lb (5.74kg). **Cartridge:** 7.62mm NATO. **Effective range:** 874.4yd (800m).

The FR-F2 is the current French sniper rifle, used by French Army and counter-terrorist units. It is a development of the 7.5mm FR-F1, first issued in 1966. Like the FR-F1, it is a bolt-action rifle with a 10-round detachable magazine and integral bipod. French Army models are fitted with a 6 x 42 scope.

The FR-F1 fired the M1936 7.5mm x 54 cartridge: one unique to France, and of little interest to potential customers outside France or French colonies. Although some were modified to fire 7.62mm NATO ammunition, it was used only by French forces.

The FR-F2 also introduced some significant changes. Apart from the inevitable change to 7.62mm caliber, it has the bipod just forward of the magazine, so the sniper can adjust it without having to move out of position. The fore-end is made of metal, rather than wood, and is covered in a matt black plastic. The barrel too, is sheathed in a plastic thermal sleeve. The idea is to minimize its infra-red signature and stop the heat from the barrel interfering with the shooter's sight picture. Designed to achieve a first-round hit on a man-size target at 766.6 yards (600m), it will group all 10 shots within 7.87in (20cm) at that range. At 218.5 yards (200m), it groups to within 1.97in (5cm).

The 6 x 42 telescopic sight has a field-of-view of 70 mils and the mount will accept any NATO-standard scope. The manufacturer, GIAT, states that the rifle will maintain its accuracy for 12,000 rounds. Like almost all sniping rifles, the butt stock can be adjusted to suit the individual soldier, and the cheek pad is also adjustable.

Right: FR-F2 with Sopelem OB 50 scope for night-firing. Any scope with a NATO baseplate attachment can be fitted.

Below: A development of the 7.5mm FR-F1, the 7.62mm FR-F2 sports a sturdy bipod mounted ahead of the 10-round magazine.

Above: The ability to adjust the butt stock and the cheek pad to suit individual needs enhances the sniper's effectiveness.

.50in Barrett rifles

Origin: USA. **Type:** Sniper rifle. **Length:** (**Model 82A1**) 60.98in (1,549mm); (**Model 90**) 45in (1,143mm); barrel length (**Model 82A1**) 29in (737mm); (**Model 90**) 29.48in (749mm). **Weight:** (**Model 82A1**) 29.77lb (13.4kg); (**Model 90**) 22.22lb (10kg). **Cartridge:** 50in Browning (12.7mm x 99). **Muzzle velocity:** 2,732ft/s (833m/s). **Feed:** (**Model 82A1**) 11-round detachable box magazine; (**Model 90**) 6-round detachable box magazine.

The Barrett .50in caliber sniper rifle is credited with a confirmed kill at 1,093 yards (1,000m) during Operation *Desert Storm*. Since the mid-1980s, several manufacturers have been providing small quantities of .50in rifles to the US Army and the Marine Corps. There was no official competition, but once the value of the .50in rifle concept had been accepted, it was likely that one company would win an order. The Barrett Model 82A1 semi-automatic rifle has emerged the winner from this process: in September 1991, the firm announced it had been awarded a US National Stock Number, and that 300 weapons had been ordered.

Against human targets, .50in weapons are obviously guaranteed to deliver massive injury and at far greater range than is possible with conventional rifle ammunition. The penetrative power of the .50 round also enables it to destroy light vehicles, aircraft and helicopters. Such rifles are also used by US Explosive Ordnance Disposal (EOD) units to destroy route denial munitions from a safe distance. Faced with a runway covered in bomblets no more than 1.96in (5cm) across, EOD personnel have found a powerful and accurate rifle to be the best solution. While 7.62mm rifles can hit 1.96in (5cm) diameter bomblets from 218.6 yards (200m) away, their lighter ammunition does not always destroy the target. The 1,000-grain .50in bullet does.

The Model 82A1 is a massive weapon over 5ft (1.5m) long. It overcomes the formidable recoil of the .50in round by using a double-baffle muzzle brake. This diverts much of the propellant gas sideways, sending a cloud of dust into the air if it is fired from dry ground. The clear signature of such weapons is an inherent

problem; without an efficient muzzle brake, the recoil would be unbearable.

In late-1991, Barrett launched a bolt-action version, designated the Model 90. This uses a bullpup layout to reduce the overall length to more manageable proportions, although some 80 per cent of the components are interchangeable. Both weapons use the Leupold & Stevens x10 scope. With long-range .50in shooting taking off as a sport in the US, the interest in these weapons seems to be increasing; although at $4,000 each, they are not cheap.

Above: A close-up study of the Leupold & Stevens x10 scope on a Model 82A1, the use of which provides range data from 1,640 to 2,624ft (500 to 800m) and references for wind-induced drift. The 11-round detachable box magazine visible houses .50in Browning ammunition.

Left: Provision of a folding bipod is all but essential if these massive weapons are to be used effectively. Weighing in at close to 30lb (13.62kg) and measuring over 5ft (1.5m) in length, their recoil when firing .50in shells is defrayed by the muzzle brake.

7.62mm Vaime Mk2 sniper rifle

Origin: Finland. **Type:** Silenced sniper rifle. **Dimensions:** Length 46.49in (1,181mm); barrel length 18.30in (465mm); suppressor length 25.98in (660mm). **Weight:** 9.08lb (4.09kg) without sights. **Cartridge:** 7.62mm x 51 subsonic. **Effective range:** 218.6yd (200m). **Feed:** 10-round box magazine.

This sniper rifle is unusual in being designed from the outset as a silenced weapon for anti-terrorist units. Developed by Oy Vaimennin Metalli Ab (Vaime) in Finland, it fires subsonic 7.62mm x 51 NATO ammunition.

The suppressor slows and cools the propellant gases. The bullet exits the barrel and passes through the suppressor, followed by the gases. They enter an expansion chamber through an aluminum baffle with four holes in it. Then the gases pass through eight further baffles, slanted at 90 degrees to each other.

Based on a Tikka bolt action receiver, the Vaime has a fast and smooth bolt action and an adjustable cheek pad. Using subsonic ammunition, it produces little recoil and about the same noise as a suppressed .22in weapon.

The US Secret Service uses the Vaime Mk2, fitting it with a Bushnell scope that has a built-in bullet drop compensator. The US Marine Corps and Navy SEALs have also experimented with the same system. In an emergency, the Vaime can be fired with full-power 7.62mm rounds.

Below: A dedicated sniping rifle, the Mk2's exterior is coated in black epoxy paint to reduce its infra-red signature.

12-bore Franchi SPAS 12

Origin: Italy. **Type:** Anti-riot shotgun. **Dimensions:** Length 37.2in (930mm); (stock folded) 28.4in (710mm); barrel 18.4in (460mm). **Weight:** 9.2lb (4.2kg). **Caliber:** 12 bore. **Rate of fire:** 250rpm (theoretical); 24-30rpm (practical).

This Special Purpose Automatic Shotgun (SPAS) was first produced in October 1979 by the firm of Luigi Franchi Development. It was based on the perception that a specific riot shotgun was needed, that shotguns then in use were largely modified sport models, and that a military/police weapon in this area was the answer.

The gun itself has a skeleton butt and a special device enabling it to be fired with one hand if the occasion dictates. Short barreled and semi-automatic, the receiver is composed of light alloy and other parts (barrel and gas cylinder) are chromed to resist corrosion.

Automatic action of the shotgun permits it to fire about four shots a second. Using standard buckshot rounds, it can put 48 pellets a second on a target at almost 44yd (40m). It uses a wide range of ammunition: buck-shot, solid slug, small pellets and tear gas rounds. With a grenade launcher fitted to the muzzle, it can fire grenades out to a maximum range of nearly 165yd (150m). A special scattering device also fits on the muzzle and produces an instantaneous spread of pellets.

The Model 12 differs slightly from the Model 11, the main differences being in the fore-end and the improved and strengthened folding stock.

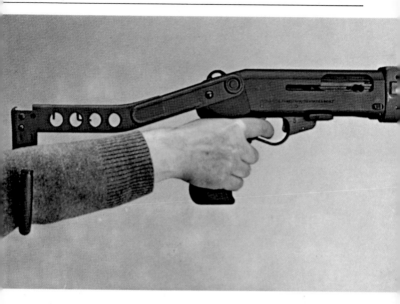

Above: Franchi Model 12 SPAS has a folding stock with a forearm rest enabling it to be fired with one hand, as shown here.

Below: SPAS Model 12 is a short-barreled semi-automatic shotgun of simple and reliable design; it can fire four rounds per second.

12-bore Ithaca 37

Origin: United States. **Type:** Police/military shotgun. **Dimensions:**
Length 18.8 to 20in (470-508mm). **Weights:** 6.5 to 7lb (2.94-3.06kg).
Caliber: 12-bore, 2¾in. **Feed:** 5- or 8-shot tubular magazine.

This shotgun is the famed basic "Featherlight" Model 37 pump action
repeater manufactured by the Ithaca Gun Company of Ithaca, New York. It is
a weapon that is uniquely free of stamped steel components, even to the trigger group.

The solid steel receiver does not have the usual ejection port on the right
because it pops empty shells straight out of the bottom. Its unique action is
centered around a dual-duty shell carrier that lifts live shells up to feed straight
into the chamber.

Its pistol-grip affords greater control while firing from the shoulder, and
makes it practical to fire from a hip position.

The type of barrel in Ithaca's "Deerslayer" model (a trade-mark of the company to indicate precision-bored cylindrical barrels for general hunting uses)
has been fitted to a combat shotgun. The objective is to provide a weapon
capable of firing rifle slugs with optimum accuracy as well as capable of handl-
ing the usual loadings. It is designated the 12-gauge DS Police Special.

A number of short-barrelled cylinder-bored configurations have been put in
use by military and police forces in the US.

12-bore Mossberg 500 ATP8

Origin: United States. **Type:** Police/military shotgun. **Dimensions:**
Length, ATP8 40.3in (1,009mm), ATP8C (pistol-grip) 30.9in (762mm);
barrel, ATP8 20.3in (308mm), ATP8C (pistol-grip) 20.3in (508mm).
Weights: ATP8 6.7lb (3.06kg), ATP8C (pistol-grip) 6.1lb (2.72kg). **Caliber:**
12-bore, 2¾ or 3in. **Magazine capacity:** 8-shot tubular.

The basic series of Mossberg 500 shotguns is specially modified for police and
military use. They have been described by some, as have other shotguns, as
"reloadable Claymores".

There are two main types — the six-shot and eight-shot models — but it is
the latter which is used by special forces. Its design is such as to ensure maximum reliability in use. It has an aluminium receiver for good balance and light
weight. A cylinder-bored barrel, which is proof-tested to full magnum loads,
provides optimum dispersion patterns and allows a variety of ammunition to
be fired.

The shotgun has twin extractors and the slide mechanism has twin guide
bars that help prevent twisting or jamming during rapid operation. A recent
addition is that the muzzle has been formed into a muzzle brake by cutting
slots in the upper surface. Gas can then be expelled in such a way as to exert
downward force, thus permitting easier pointing. In its pistol-grip form, the
Mossberg ATP8 is extremely compact and can thus be stowed more easily inside vehicles.

There is an almost infinite variety of options available. Latest model is the
Bullpup 12 shot-gun version of the Mossberg 500. This consists of the basic
Model 500 action inside a totally new framework made from impact-resistant
thermoplastic material.

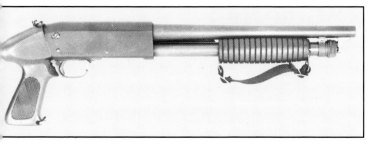

Above: The Ithaca Model 37 'Stakeout' is so compact (the barrel is just 13.3in (336mm) long) that it can be hidden under a topcoat.

Above: Ithaca Model 37 M&P shotgun with long, 8-round magazine.

Above: The US Mossberg company makes a series of 12-gauge pump-action shotguns for police, military and sporting use.

RPG series

Origin: Soviet Union. **Type:** Anti-tank rocket launchers. **Dimensions:**
Length RPG-7V (less projectile) 38.5in (990mm); RPG-18 (folded) 27.75in
(705mm), (extended) 39.4in (1,000mm). **Weight:** RPG-7V (less projectile)
15.42lb (7kg), RPG-18 (complete) 8.8lb (4kg). **Projectile:** RPG-7V weight
4.96lb (2.25kg); diameter 3.35in (85mm); RPG-18 weight 5.5lb (2.5kg);
diameter 2.5in (64mm). **Muzzle velocity:** RPG-7V 984f/s (300m/s);
RPG-18 374f/s (114m/s). **Effective range:** RPG-7V 328yd (300m); RPG-18
219yd (200m). **Armor penetration:** RPG-7V 12in (320mm).

The Soviet Army has placed great emphasis on anti-tank defence since its
traumatic experiences at the hands of the German Panzer troops during World
War II. For many years the standard anti-armor weapon of the Soviet infantry
and marines has been the RPG-7V (RPG = *Reaktivniy Protivotankovyi
Granatomet* (rocket, anti-tank grenade launcher)). This weapon fires a projectile whose internal rocket motor ignites a short distance from the muzzle, sus-
taining flight out to about 550yd (500m).

The HEAT warhead has good anti-armor performance, being capable of
penetrating 12.6in (320mm) of conventional armor. However, the large, slow-

Above: RPG-7 (this is a Chinese version) is a small weapon which has proved very popular with terrorists around the world.

Left: Soldier inserts the grenade into the muzzle of the launcher. Grenade weighs 4.96lb (2.25kg), launcher 15.42lb (7kg).

Below: RPG-7 in firing position. The missile is reasonably accurate, but is very sensitive and erratic in cross-winds.

flying projectile is extremely susceptible to cross-winds and its accuracy depends to a very large degree upon the skill of the operator in estimating wind effects. The standard optical sight is frequently supplemented by the NSP-2 (IR) night sight. There is also a folding version, designated RPG-7D, which was originally intended for use by airborne troops.

Both RPG-7V and RPG-7D are standard issue for Soviet and Warsaw Pact forces, and are also widely used by Third World forces and a number of terrorist organisations. Even in the hands of unskilled and illiterate troops they are highly effective against bunkers and buildings, vehicles of all types, and even under certain favourable circumstances, helicopters, but within the cross-wind limitation described above.

A new weapon, designated RPG-16, has recently appeared with Soviet Paratroop units, which appears to be a product-improved RPG-7V. This weapon has a permanently fitted bipod, and the rocket is not carried on the weapon, as is the case with RPG-7V. It has been suggested that the RPG-16 projectile may work on the double-warhead principle: the first shaped-charge makes the initial penetration of the target's armor, following which the second charge is fired through to exploit the damage caused by the first.

The RPG-18 is a disposable light anti-armor weapon (LAW), which has just entered service. The launcher is a telescopic, extruded-alloy tube, which is 27.75in (705mm) long in the carrying mode. The launcher is pulled out to its full length of 39.4in (1,000mm) before firing. The launch tube has a series of simple drawings, giving the operating instructions, an idea apparently derived from the US M72 LAW.

Above: Afghan mujahideen with an RPG-16, a product-improved RPG-7, captured from occupying Soviet forces.

Below: Vietnamese soldier with an RPG-2, the earlier version of the RPG-7. Thousands of the RPG-2/7 family are in use.

LAW80 Light anti-tank weapon

Orign: United Kingdom. **Type:** Portable anti-tank weapon. **Dimensions:** Length 3.3ft (1m) folded; 4.95ft (1.5m) extended; caliber 3.7in (94mm). **Weights:** Carry 21.1lb (9.6kg); shoulder 19.3lb (8.8kg). **Penetration:** Greater than 2.4in (600mm) of armor. **Range:** 22-500yd (20-500m).

The LAW80 is a one-shot, low cost, disposable, short-range anti-tank weapon system. It is designed to permit the operator to engage main battle tanks over short ranges with the high probability of a hit.

It is stored and transported holding 24 launchers and issued directly to the user; it is fully man-portable with personal weapons and pack with carrying handle and shoulder sling.

A spotting rifle is used with the system, which contains five rounds — which can be fired without revealing position. The 9mm ammunition, which is matched ballistically to the main projectile, is marked by a tracer and by a flash head to record a hit on a hard target. The operator can select and fire the main projectile at any time.

The LAW80 sight has its own sliding protective cover. End caps provide sealing for the tubes against immersion, despite the fact that the projectile itself is sealed. After removal of the end caps, the HEAT projectile is extended rearwards from the outer tube. The launch tube is automatically locked into position and the sight erected.

The gunner then only has to select "arm" on a lever to use the trigger to fire either the spotting rifle or the projectile. A non-electric system made up of a percussion cap in the launcher connected by a flash tube to the rocket igniter fires the projectile.

Below: The LAW80, a lightweight, man-portable, short-range anti-tank weapon, also has a role in special forces operations.

Above: LAW80 has a built-in, disposable, 5-round spotting-rifle. Bullets are matched ballistically to main round.

A HEAT warhead and its flying unit make up the forward part of the projectile, and there is a double-ogive nose-switch, which also provides the optimum standoff distance from the target. At the rear of the projectile the composite aluminium and filament-wound motor-case has an extruded vane propellant. Four fins are mounted on the rear of the motor.

In the British armed forces the weapon is used by infantry, supporting arms, Royal Marines, and the RAF Regiment. Some special operations personnel claim the LAW80 is used as anything but an anti-tank weapon; they describe it as a "super bullet", and as a device that comes under the heading of an "attention-getter" for tanks.

Below: British Marines storm ashore from a landing-craft. One carries LAW80 with ease showing its excellent man-portability.

Stinger, FIM-92A

Origin: United States. **Type:** Man-portable air defence missile.
Dimensions: Missile length 60in (1,524mm); body diameter 2.75in
(69.8mm). **Weights:** Launch 24lb (10.9kg); package 35lb (15.8kg).
Propulsion: Atlantic Research. **Guidance:** Optical aiming, IR homing.
Range: In excess of 3.1 miles (5km). **Flight speed:** About Mach 2.
Warhead: High explosive.

This successor to the first-generation Redeye missile went to the field in
Europe in 1982. Stinger has a much improved infra-red guidance system over
the Redeye that permits effective attack from all angles, whereas Redeye was
limited to a stern chase. Stinger also has greater resistance to counter-
measures and incorporates an IFF system for positive identification of hostile
aircraft, a capability considered essential by friendly aircrew who are increasingly apprehensive of the sophisticated air defence weapons issued to their
own troops. The IFF device, about the size of the average canteen, is attached
to the firer's belt. The missile is issued as a certified round of ammunition in a
disposable sealed launching tube, which is attached to the gripstock tracking
unit containing the missile's controls and pre-launch electronics.

To improve its effectiveness and cope with ECM of the future, an advanced
seeker called Stinger POST (for Passive Optical Seeker Technique) has been
developed. It was introduced on the production line with the Fiscal 1983 buy.
This version operates in both the ultraviolet and the infra-red spectra. The improved missile reached the field in Fiscal 1987.

Stingers are being used by the anti-Soviet forces in Afghanistan with, by all
accounts, deadly effect. The Soviets are now fighting that war at greater and
safer distances . . . fearing this weapon in the hands of the mujahideen.

**Right: The US Stinger man-portable, air defense missile has proved
effective in the Falklands and in Afghanistan.**

**Below: In conventional war the radioman is needed to prevent own
aircraft being hit, but would not be required in SF operations.**

Blowpipe/Javelin

Origin: United Kingdom. **Type:** Surface-to-air missile (SAM). **Canister:** Length 54.7in (1.390m); weight: 48.3lb (21.9kg). **Missile:** Length 54.7in (1,390mm); diameter: 3in (76mm). **Rocket motor:** Two-stage, solid-fuel. **Effective range:** 3 to 3.7 miles (5 to 6km). **Flight speed:** Supersonic.

Blowpipe is a lightweight, supersonic, self-contained SAM system, currently used by 14 armed forces in 10 countries. The system worked well in the 1982 South Atlantic war (it was deployed by both sides) and a number of successes were recorded. It has also found its way to Afghanistan, being reported in use by the mujahideen from 1983 onwards.

The basic Blowpipe system comprises two units. The first is a sealed launch canister containing the missile, which is treated in the supply system simply as a round of ammunition. Second is the aiming unit, a self-contained pack. To prepare for action the aiming unit is clipped to the launch canister, and the complete system is then put on the operator's shoulder. When the operator has acquired the target and confirmed it as hostile he pulls the trigger, generating electrical impulses which energise the thermal battery, powering up the aiming unit and one second later firing the missile motor. The missile is ejected from the tube by the first-stage motor and, when well clear of the operator, the second-stage ignites. The operator then 'gathers' the missile and guides it to the target using a thumb-stick, which transmits signals by a radio link to the missile.

The latest service version is the Javelin, which uses the Blowpipe missile, but with a more powerful motor which significantly reduces the time of flight. The aiming unit is externally similar to that for Blowpipe, but houses a new control system, using semi-automatic command line-of-sight (SACLOS) guidance in which all the operator needs to do is keep the cross-wires in his sight on the target. The TV camera in the aiming unit tracks the flare in the missile tail and compares this with the signals from the sight; any mismatch is converted into an error correction signal which is transmitted to the missile.

Javelin is man-portable but installations are under development for both soft-skinned and armored vehicles.

Above: The Blowpipe air defense missile has been sold to many overseas customers, including special forces.

Left: Successor to Blowpipe, Javelin is much faster, with **SACLOS** guidance system, greatly reducing the load on the operator.

SA-7 Grail

Origin: Soviet Union. **Type:** Surface-to-air missile (SAM). **Launcher:** Length 53.25in (1.35m); weight: 23.4lb (10.6kg). **Missile:** Length 48.8in (1,240mm); diameter 2.75in (70mm); weight 20.3lb (9.2kg). **Rocket motor:** Three-stage, solid-fuel. **Effective height:** SA-7A maximum 9,843ft (3,000m); minimum 164ft (50m). SA-7B maximum 16,000ft (5km); minimum 164ft (50m). **Maximum speed:** SA-7A 994mph (1,600km/h). SA-7B 1,242mph (2,000km/h).

Originally called *Strela* (Arrow) in the West, this widely used SAM is now designated the SA-7, and has the NATO reporting name of 'Grail'. It is a simple infantry weapon and originally had great similarity with the US Redeye, sharing many of the latter's notorious shortcomings. Most important of these was the inability of the uncooled PbS infra-red seeker to lock onto any heat source on a fixed-wing target, other than the tailpipe. This limited engagements to 'tail chases', which was obviously tactically unacceptable. They could, however, hit helicopters from almost any angle.

Right: Soviet air defense missileman launches an SA-7 from the rear hatch of a BMP APC during a training exercise.

Below: SA-7 is used by Warsaw Pact military forces, Soviet client states and numerous terrorist organizations.

The SA-7 missile is essentially a tube with a dual-thrust solid-fuel motor, steered by canard fins. The operator merely aims the launcher at the target using the open sight and takes the first pressure on the trigger, which switches on the thermal battery. He then waits for an audible warning and the red light to turn green, which indicate that the seeker has locked-on; he then applies the full trigger pressure. The boost charge fires and burns out before the tail of the missile has cleared the tube. At a safe distance the sustainer motor ignites, accelerating the missile to about Mach 1.5.

The 5.5lb (2.5kg) warhead has a smooth fragmentation casing, and is fitted with both impact and grazing fuzes. The original warhead was lethal only against small aircraft and in the Yom Kippur war almost half the Israeli A-4s hit by SA-7s returned to base.

An improved missile (SA-7B) has been in production since 1972 with augmented propulsion giving a higher speed and better maximum operating height. It also has an infra-red filter to screen out decoys and the prominent nose ring on the front-end of the launcher is believed to house a much better guidance system.

There are probably 50,000 missiles and almost as many launchers in service, large numbers of them in use by terrorists.

THE MOST fundamental questions concerning special forces are why are they needed, who are they, and what do they do? They are, after all, expensive to select, train and equip, and their very élitism and aura of secrecy tend to induce envy in other sections of their armies and fear in governments. Nevertheless, many countries now see little alternative but to have such groups.

There have long been special units in many forces, which have set particular conditions for entry. These have varied from simple matters such as height for 'guards' units, to a very high degree of physical fitness for parachute and marine units. Starting in the late 1950s, however, the needs of counter-revolutionary warfare (CRW) gave rise to a requirement for units with a high degree of skill and specialization in dealing with specific threats. This expanded slowly in the 1960s until the spread of international terrorism and the prevalence of hijacking, kidnapping, random bombings and murders forced a marked upsurge in the numbers and size of special forces.

Special forces tend to operate in the area that lies between the police and the 'heavy' infantry. Some countries have tried to fill this gap by developing special sections of the police. In West Germany, for example, the special force GSG-9 (GSG = Grenzschutzgruppe = Border Defence Group) is part of the State Border Police, directed by the Federal Ministry of the Interior. In the United Kingdom the equivalent is the Special Air Service (SAS) Regiment, which is a unit of the British Army, although various police forces have started to create their own armed squads, albeit dealing with lower level situations than would be dealt with by the SAS.

These forces operate in situations where police cannot, either for legal or training reasons. They are always at a high degree of readiness and are

Below: Federal German Police lined up for anti-riot duties with helmets, shields and body armor, invaluable for today's police forces.

trained and equipped to deal with a wide range of contingencies. These can be conveniently divided into three levels. At the first, or lowest, level is the operation against a small number of terrorists in a fairly confined target such as an aircraft, ship or single building, and located either in the home country or in a friendly territory with full cooperation from the authorities. Examples of such operations are the British SAS rescue of the hostages in the Iranian Embassy siege (1980) and the West German rescue of the hostages in the hijacking at Mogadishu (1977). The second level of special force operations are those involving an attack against larger targets at long distances and in which the enemy are either terrorists supported by regular troops or regular troops themselves. Examples of this type are the Israeli rescue of the hijacked hostages at Entebbe (1976) and the US Operation *Eagle Claw* in which the Delta Force attempted to rescue the US hostages in Teheran (1980). Finally, there are the third level operations in a proper war

Above: Black-clad special forces soldier abseiling with MP5. He must be at instant readiness for long periods for operations anywhere in the world.

setting where special forces act as a specialist part of the regular military forces. Examples of this are the US raid to release the prisoners of war held at Son Tay in 1970 and the British SAS and SBS (Special Boat Squadron, an élite element of the Royal Marines) operations in the South Atlantic war of 1982.

General tactics

Perhaps the highest profile activity of special forces is hostage rescue. For some years after aircraft hijacking was invented it appeared to be an insuperable tactic, and the balance of advantage seemed to lie irretrievably with the terrorist. At first confined to aircraft, hijacking has since taken place on trains, buses and even ships. However, the authorities in most countries have managed to develop suitable responses, which have led to a marked decrease, although the complexity of modern transportation systems, coupled with the difficulty of maintaining the necessary high level of vigilance, means that such crimes remain a constant possibility.

In all counter-terrorist operations the first essential is intelligence; indeed, good intelligence should enable incidents to be prevented altogether. Long-term, in-depth intelligence is necessary and it would appear that a great number of military and police authorities now exchange intelligence on an international scale, which has proved to be a major deterrent to many would-be terrorists. Once an incident has started, however, there are two requirements: first, to gather all possible intelligence on the group involved, their personalities, motives, tactics, doctrines and determination, leading to an anaylsis of their

Below: Hostage takers increasingly hide in buildings in urban areas, giving rescuers considerable problems in achieving rapid and effective entry.

strengths and weaknesses. Second, to establish everything possible about the actual incident itself: how many are involved, what arms they have, what their contacts are, how many hostages there are and so on. From all this contingency plans can be prepared to cover various possible situations and then it is a matter of waiting.

When the actual operation takes place the essentials are surprise, determination and rapid, coordinated action. Overwhelming force is seldom necessary; indeed, in many situations (eg, an attack on an aircraft) it may not be physically possible to get too many men into the target area. Two good examples of the tactics involved are the Israeli rescue mission to Entebbe and the British breaking of the Iranian Embassy siege in London.

Entebbe Operation
The Israeli rescue operation at Entebbe was a classic of its kind, showing the ability of special forces to react quickly to unexpected crises, to make rapid but flexible plans and

Above: SAS 'enemy' (left) is captured in a recent desert exercise. The SAS were formed during World War II in the North African desert campaign.

to operate at considerable distance from their home base. The crisis began at 1210 hours on 27 June 1976, when an Air France Airbus (Flight AF 139) was hijacked en route from Athens to Paris. The flight had started in Tel Aviv and there were many Jews among the 254 passengers. The pilot pressed the 'hijack alert' button as he turned for Benghazi under orders from the leader of the combined Baader-Meinhof/Palestinian group, led by a German, Wilfried Boese. The aircraft refuelled at Benghazi and then flew to its destination Entebbe, Uganda, which was at that time under the erratic rule of 'Field Marshal' Idi Amin.

Israeli planners had many problems, including shortage of time, paucity of information, and distance. There was also the problem of the non-Jewish hostages. Some of these problems solved themselves. The hijackers released the non-Jewish hostages (although the Air France crew insisted that they stay with the remaining Jewish hostages), intelligence on Entebbe and the situation there began to trickle in, and Kenya agreed to the use of Nairobi airport.

The rescue plan was approved by the Israeli Prime Minister early on 3 July and a dress-rehearsal was carried out later than morning, taking just 55 minutes from aircraft-touch-down to take-off with simualted rescued hostages. At 1600 hours that afternoon four C-130 aircraft took off for the flight to Entebbe; they were followed some two hours later by two Boeing 707 aircraft one of which was a flying command post, the other a mobile hospital. The hospital aircraft flew to Nairobi airport but, in the event, its facilities were not needed.

The four C-130s landed at Entebbe at 0001 hours, the first going straight to the control tower, which was captured before the airfield landing lights could be switched off. Another party blew up a number of Ugandan Air Force MiG fighters in a noisy diversion (which also ensured that the fighters could not follow the Israelis after they took off for home). Another group set up ambushes on the approach road to the airport to ensure that no Ugandan rescue forces could interrupt the operation.

The preliminaries successfully

completed, the signal was given to assault the terminal building where the hostages were held. The terrorist leader behaved somewhat indecisively and was killed as he returned into the building, his German female accomplice being shot outside the building. Inside the terminal the assaulting troops yelled at the hostages to keep down but three hostages were shot by stray bullets as the last of the terrorists were being killed. The terrorists disposed of, the released hostages were rapidly shepherded out to the waiting C-130s, and at this point the assault force

Below: A very cheerful C-130 pilot is thanked by hostages who had lived through days of terror in Entebbe, held by a PLO group supported by Idi Amin.

commander, Lieutenant-Colonel 'Yoni' Netanyahu, was shot and killed by a single shot from a Ugandan soldier in a nearby building.

The first C-130 took off at 0045 hours and the fourth at 0054 hours. The cost of the whole operation was one member of the rescue force killed and three wounded; three hostages were killed during the assault and one, Mrs Dora Bloch, who had earlier been taken to a Ugandan hospital, was murdered by Ugandans in revenge for the humiliating débâcle. All the terrorists were killed, together with 20 Ugandans.

Iranian Embassy Siege
A second example of a classic special force operation was the 1980 rescue of the hostages in the Iranian Embassy in London. Its impact lay in the

fact that it took place in full view of the media and was the first public display of the long-suspected prowess of the British Special Air Service (SAS).

The Embassy was taken over at 1130 hours on 30 April 1980 by six terrorists armed with three 9mm automatic pistols, one 0.38in revolver and some hand grenades. The six men were seeking independence for Arabistan, an area of southern Iran, which has a long record of resistance to northern domination. This was an internal Iranian dispute, in which the British had no involvement whatsoever. There were 29 people in the Embassy at the time of the takeover (4 British and 22 Iranian, 3 of the latter escaping in the first few minutes). Having stated their demands and set a deadline (1200 hours, 1 May) the

terrorists found themselves involved in continuous contact with the police, discussing the release of sick hostages, postponement of deadlines and passing messages to and from third parties. This was all part of a recognised police gambit to establish and maintain contact, to set up relationships between police officers and individual terrorists, and to begin the long process of wearing the terrorists down. Meanwhile every element of the exterior of the building was being investigated in minute detail to establish possible entry routes.

By the third day there had been

Below: 4 July 1976 and an Israeli Air Force C-130 Hercules lands a Lod Airport, carrying the hostages who had been freed in the spectacular raid on Entebbe.

Above left: The image of the SAS that shook the world. Clad in black, wearing respirators and NBC hoods, and armed with H&K MP5's, they prepare to enter.

Left: London Iranian Embassy siege; a hostage flees across the balconies. The speed and efficiency of the 11-minute rescue operation stunned watchers.

Above: London firemen ready to extinguish fires started accidentally during the rescue. The position of the Iranians in Embassy Row is clearly shown.

numerous contacts and the terrorists agreed to release two hostages in-return for a radio broadcast giving a statement of their aims. Both were achieved and the police sent in a

Above: After its success in World War II the SAS was disbanded, only to be reformed in the 1950s to fight terrorists in Malaya. They proved as successful in jungle as they had been in the African desert.

meal. The siege continued through Days 4 and 5, but on Day 6 the terrorists were noticeably more edgy and at 1330 hours the leader shot and killed one of the Embassy staff, the body being pushed out onto the pavement at 1900 hours.

The SAS assault took place just 26 minutes later, using 12 men, in the usual SAS four-man teams. Everything that could be done to heighten the impact was done: the soldiers were dressed from head to foot in black, even including anti-gas respirators, and looked extremely menacing. They were armed with a variety of weapons, including Heckler & Koch MP5 carbines and Browning 9mm pistols. Tear gas was used together with 'stun' grenades, while the explosion of the shaped charges added to the noise and confusion. The SAS men had, naturally, pored over the plans of the 50-room building in

minute detail and had spent many hours studying the photographs of the hostages. Just before the assault started the police spoke to the terrorists on the telephone to distract their attention at the critical moment.

One element of the assault was made from the roof, the men abseiling down ropes at the front and rear of the building, the second from the balcony of the adjacent building. At the rear the third soldier became entangled in the rope and had to be cut down, falling onto a balcony. At the front the men climbed onto a balcony of the Iranian Embassy, placed a shaped charge and entered. Inside there was chaos, with noise of firearms, flashes, bangs, shouts and yells. The terrorists managed to wound a few of the hostages before they were all killed by the SAS, except for one who managed to hide among the rescued hostages for a few minutes before being arrested.

The entire operation took 11 minutes and established the SAS's reputation globally. It also delivered an inescapable message to other terrorists: that any future adventure in the UK would be dealt with in a similar manner.

MODERN ammunition manufacturers offer a bewildering and ever-expanding variety of cartridges. There are bullets intended for every kind of game, animal and human; and bullets for long-range sniping or close-quarter battle. Many ingenious solutions have been employed to maximize the damage caused by a single round. Yet by a curious twist of international law, soldiers are banned from using them against each other. A series of international agreements signed at the turn of the century banned the use of exploding or expanding bullets in military conflicts. During the Boer War, British soldiers had suffered horrific injuries from soft-nosed bullets normally used by the Boer farmers for hunting. Boers captured with such ammunition in their pockets were often summarily executed.

In the name of humanity, the world's major armies agreed to restrict soldiers to the use of cartridges with a full metal jacket covering the lead bullet. A few years later, these same armies were embroiled in World War I and introduced mustard gas and flamethrowers. Later inventions have included napalm and nuclear weapons, but the restrictions on small arms ammunition remain in force. It is still a disciplinary offence for British soldiers to cut notches in the heads of their bullets to increase their wounding effect.

Elite Forces soldiers are in a different position. They are frequently engaged in anti-terrorist operations — and the Geneva and Hague conventions only apply to conventional military conflict. Criminals and terrorists enjoy no such protection.

Handgun ammunition

Elite Forces personnel are the only soldiers likely to use a handgun as an offensive weapon rather than for self-defense. Working in plain clothes during anti-terrorist operations or fighting in a confined space during hostage rescues, a handgun is often the best weapon for the job. Unfortunately, most western armies have adopted a standard pistol cartridge that is ill-suited to their requirements. The NATO standard 9mm Parabellum cartridge weighs 115 grains and complies with the international agreements described above. Fired from typical western pistols such as the Browning High-Power or the Beretta 92, it is accurate, reliable and controllable. Yet its performance, while adequate on the battlefield, is not ideal for those Elite Forces soldiers fighting terrorists.

A single hit — or succession of hits — might well cause fatal injury, but this is not always enough. A soldier storming an airliner full of hostages needs to kill his terrorist opponent instantly. A fanatic terrorist may well be able to detonate a bomb, lob a grenade or shoot into the crowd despite being hit himself.

9mm bullets are used by many law

Below: Some current shotgun cartridges. Of the rifled slugs in the bottom row, numbers 1, 3 and 5 are tungsten penetrators.

Above: More typical shotgun cartridges. SPAS round (right) is a discarding sabot tungsten carbide slug which can penetrate the side of an APC!

enforcement agencies in Europe and the USA. Many are designed to mushroom on impact, creating the maximum wounding effect. Silvertip hollowpoints are popular in the USA; London's Metropolitan Police use a semi-jacketed semi-wadcutter that expands and cuts an enlarged wound channel. Nevertheless, there is strong evidence that to stop an enemy immediately, a 9mm bullet has to strike the head or the spine, or shatter the tibia. The US Special Forces are following the Federal Bureau of Investigation (FBI) and adopting new, larger handgun cartridges which are more likely to deliver the sort of instantaneous knock-down they require.

In 1986, eight FBI agents fought a five-minute gun battle with two armed criminals in Miami. One of the felons was put down quickly, but the other shot five of the FBI men, slaying two of them, before being killed himself: this was despite the fact that at the very beginning of the battle, the criminal was struck by a 9mm Silvertip that passed through his arm and penetrated his chest cavity. He was shot repeatedly in the ensuing gun battle, but no single strike inflicted enough damage to stop him immediately. He was not on drugs; he was just a very determined individual who forced himself to keep going.

The FBI promptly reviewed its weapons and tactics. It adopted a heavier, 147-grain 9mm bullet that would penetrate deep enough to have killed the Miami felon outright with the first round. But after further study, it has now abandoned the 9mm cartridge altogether and issues its agents with Smith & Wesson pistols firing a new 10mm round. Heckler & Koch have now launched a version of their famous MP5 sub-machine gun, chambered for this powerful projectile that delivers double the muzzle energy of standard 9mm loads. With better penetration and stopping power, there is little doubt that the 10mm cartridge is a step forward. However, although tested by the military, the 10mm remains a lawman's bullet: US Special Forces are thinking even bigger.

In 1991, US Special Operations Command invited Heckler & Koch and Colt to develop a new pistol for Special Forces personnel. It is to be chambered for .45in ACP: the big-bore cartridge still very popular in the USA and only recently replaced as the Army's service pistol round. In some respects, the wheel has turned full circle: the US Army insisted on .45in caliber pistols some 90 years ago.

Standard .45in Ball ammunition weighs twice as much as 9mm ammunition and inflicts substantially more damage. Police and hunting loads — such as the 185-grain hollowpoint — are even more effective. From a military standpoint, the .45in cartridge suffers from one major disadvantage: it is a chunky, dustbin-size round and only six or seven can be fitted into a magazine. Comparable 9mm pistols can be loaded with twice as many rounds, or even more. However, the enduring reputation of the .45in cartridge has led several manufacturers to introduce new .45in pistols with double-row magazines capable of holding a dozen rounds or more. The only drawback with guns like the .45in Glock 17 or the Para-Ordnance 14-round version of the Colt M1911 is that the grip is correspondingly fatter. You need big paws to grasp it comfortably.

In 1990 Smith & Wesson launched a new cartridge: the .40in Smith & Wesson. Two years later, at least six other companies are manufacturing pistols to fire it. It is similar in performance to the more moderate 10mm cartridges — like the FBI's "10mm Lite"; but being externally closer to a 9mm cartridge, the .40in S&W can be stacked into a magazine in similar quantities. Currently all the rage with US law enforcement agencies, it is another possible choice for Special Forces units seeking an improvement on 9mm Parabellum.

While NATO forces have been gradually standardizing their small arms, the Soviet Union and its former client states in Eastern Europe were also using a common range of ammunition. However, the Soviets adopted a very different approach to that of western nations. The Makarov and Stechkin pistols fire the 9mm Makarov cartridge, which is smaller than 9mm Parabellum and marginally less effective. The Soviet forces have never displayed any interest in hollowpoints, semi-wadcutters or other western-type bullets. The Soviet Army has never regarded handguns as much more than last-ditch defensive weapons: a back-up for vehicle crews, but not a primary weapon. The only significant alternative from standard 9mm Makarov ammunition is a down-loaded version which has a subsonic muzzle velocity. This is intended for the silenced Stechkin used by Soviet forces.

During the 1980s, the Soviets manufactured the diminutive PSM pistol in 5.45mm caliber. This tiny round is usually described as an ineffective cartridge with similar performance to that of the .22in Long Rifle round used for rabbit or varmint shooting. Because it was never exported outside the Soviet Union, the PSM remained an enigma — an apparently ineffective weapon adopted by an army which has always been equipped with top-quality small arms, whatever its other shortcomings. However, recent tests on a PSM have revealed a sinister dimension to this otherwise second-rate weapon. The 5.45mm round penetrates body armor better than 9mm Parabellum, .45in ACP or .357in Magnum for that matter. Its steel core and narrow cross-section enable it to punch through many layers of Kevlar.

Rifle ammunition

With the conspicuous exception of Germany, all major western armies now issue their infantry with a 5.56mm caliber rifle. The US forces are armed with M16A2s (soon to be upgraded to M16A3 standard); the French have the FA MAS; the British have the SA80 and many other countries have bought either M16s or the Austrian Steyr AUG.

Elite forces soldiers have had a mixed reaction for these weapons over the last 20 years or so. A weapon like the M16 is very light, as is its ammunition: this weight-saving is extremely important to Special Forces patrols. It is quicker to train recruits to shoot well with a weapon like the M16 than an FN FAL. Yet there is no doubt that the 5.56mm cartridge is less effective than the 7.62mm round it replaced. As some American servicemen lamented the demise of their M14, so some British soldiers still prefer the SLR.

British elite forces units have used the M16 from Borneo to Northern Ireland, but its reputation — and that

Below: Pistol rounds varying from .22 (bottom right) to .44 caliber (second from right, bottom), and from roundnose (third from left, bottom) to Splat polymer/metal mix (top, fifth from left, upper).

of the 5.56mm bullet — was dented by one incident in the Falklands. A Royal Marine patrol was engaged in a sudden battle with Argentinian troops. A Royal Marine shot an Argentinian soldier in the chest four times using an M16. The Argentinian still managed to raise his 7.62mm FN FAL and put a round through the Marine's leg. It was widely felt at the time that if the Marine had had an SLR rather than an M16, his target would have gone down and stayed down.

The 5.56mm bullet was designed to be effective at the sort of distance infantry units are likely to fire on each other: about 300 to 400 yards (274.5 to 366m). Only in the open space of the desert are infantrymen likely to see each other at much longer ranges. Targets beyond this distance are to be engaged with machine guns. While this arrangement makes sense for soldiers who fight from armored personnel carriers, it is less than ideal for elite forces.

During the Gulf War, the US Navy SEAL teams made extensive use of match-grade M14s and Remington sniper rifles, both chambered for the old 7.62mm cartridge. It may be obsolete for modern mechanized infantry, but for small units that need to hit their targets hard, the 7.62mm round is still in business. Skilled snipers, using top-quality ammunition, can achieve head shots at 659 yards (600m) and first-round hits on a man-sized target at up to 1,093 yards (1,000m).

Elite forces around the world continue to experiment with new sniper rifles, and new rifle cartridges. Several other calibers are regularly used by military snipers, including .300in Winchester Magnum and larger rounds chosen for their armor-piercing ability. We are familiar with the TV image of the hijacker waving his pistol about in the cockpit of an airliner. Several elite forces units (and police forces) have experimented with sniper rifles that could penetrate the aircraft and kill the terrorist from several hundred yards away. The largest rifles used by Special Forces fire .50in caliber bullets: 700-grain monsters that can penetrate armored cars.

US Special Forces use several types

Above: Used by many special forces Glaser rounds (l to r — 7.62mm, .44 Magnum, .38, 9mm) are designed for stopping power. Nintey percent of those shot by such rounds die.

of .50in caliber rifle and the British SAS has tested them for all manner of tasks. One good shot with a .50in caliber rifle could knock out a $50 million fighter-bomber from a firing point over a mile (1.6km) from the runway. Modern armies depend on complex communications networks which could easily be disrupted in a similar way. Headquarters units do have attached personnel for immediate defense, but a sniper with a .50in caliber weapon could destroy radio vehicles from a safe distance. The first .50in caliber sniper rifles used the original M2 Browning machine gun cartridge, but now the concept has become more accepted, specialist .50in caliber rifle ammunition is available, offering far better performance. Armor-piercing incendiary ammunition from a .50in caliber rifle poses a major threat to lightly-armored military vehicles. Such big-caliber rifles have the capability to destroy, or — equally useful for Special Forces — disable aircraft and helicopters. The .50in caliber round has an invaluable combination of precision and lethality.

Large-caliber rifle rounds have another valuable use: the rapid disposal of bombs and sub-munitions. Many air forces use sub-munitions to attack airfields; littering the runway with explosive devices that would take days to clear by conventional methods. A few well-trained riflemen armed with something like a McMillan .50in caliber can destroy the bomblets from a safe distance.

AHMED Shah Masood is one of the most successful commanders of the Afghan resistance. His brave and resourceful leadership led the Mujahideen to call him the *Lion of the Panjsher*. Many Soviet offensives were launched into his area of operations, but none succeeded in destroying him or his followers. So the Soviets tried another tack. The KGB and its Afghan equivalent, the *Khad*, recruited a double-agent inside Masood's camp and sent him to assassinate the

guerrilla leader with a Soviet purpose-built silence pistol.

Fortunately for Masood, this particular double-agent was doubly treacherous. He was working for the resistance all along and the Soviet's secret murder weapon was revealed to the West for the first time. He had been given a twin-barrelled pistol, one barrel above the other, which fired a 7.62mm bullet from a special cartridge case. The case contained baffles that slowed down the propellant gas,

performing the function of a silencer. Utterly silent in operation, and able to be slipped unobtrusively into a trouser pocket, this sinister weapon is manufactured only for KGB and Soviet elite forces' use.

The US Army had an equivalent weapon in Vietnam. There, Special Forces personnel taking part in such operations as the *Phoenix* program (the selective assassination of Viet Cong agents), were issued with a High-Standard .22in semi-automatic

fitted with a highly effective integral silencer.

Elite forces units do not only use silenced weapons for assassination of individual targets. The Soviet *Spetsnaz*, in particular, have silenced versions of the Stechkin 9mm machine-pistol which were used in the assault on the Afghan Presidential Palace in 1979. They also used a suppressor fitted to 7.62mm AKM rifles for ambushes of Mujahideen groups high in the barren mountains of central Afghanistan.

Although sometimes used interchangeably, the terms "silencer" and "suppressor" have different meanings. Firing a gun produces two main sounds: the "crack" of a bullet travelling at supersonic speed; and the "thump" of compressed propellant gas expanding as it emerges from the muzzle, creating a sound wave as it does so. A suppressor is a device that quietens the muzzle report by dispersing and slowing down the gas behind the bullet. Generally a tube, wider than the barrel, it is divided into many compartments which may be filled with gauze. The bullet passes up the barrel, while the following gas is obstructed in its travel and loses its velocity.

By muffling the noise at the muzzle and eliminating muzzle flash, a suppressor conceals the firer's position. A small ambush party of *Spetznas* could thus engage a large group of guerrillas and then slip away, without its location being compromised in any way.

Most major firearms manufacturers who produce weapons for elite forces offer suppressed and/or silenced versions of their guns. Only a few pubish precise performance details. Heckler & Koch quote the noise level within 6.6ft (2m) of the muzzle of the 7.62mm 63 rifle as 158-168dB depending on

Left: Silenced rifles are being used increasingly by special forces. Vaime of Finland produces this sniper rifle, as well as silencer attachments for other weapons, which reduces the sound of 7.62/5.56mm weapons to that of 0.22in rimfire.

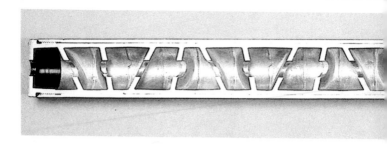

Above: An internal view of a Vaime screw-on silencer attachment. The series of baffles not only greatly reduces sound, but also eliminates muzzle-flash and reduces recoil.

Below: Heckler & Koch G3 7.62mm rifle fitted with a silencer attachment, intended mainly for use on ranges to reduce noise disturbances to local residents.

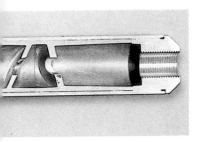

Bottom: The Chinese 7.62mm Type 64 SMG is unique in that it is designed and built as a silenced weapon; in every other case normal SMGs are fitted with silencer attachments.

exactly where you are standing. With H&K's suppressor fitted, there is an average reduction of 16dB. Since a drop of 10dB halves the noise level, this is obviously a useful bit of kit.

A bullet travelling faster than the speed of sound — about 1,082ft/s (330m/s), depending on altitude — will create a sound wave. Some low-powered pistol ammunition does not reach such a speed; but most military pistol, and all rifle rounds do. A true silencer is a device that reduces the velocity of the bullet to a subsonic level, preventing the tell-tale "crack" as it passes through the air. This is usually achieved by drilling holes in the barrel that bleed off some of the gas, reducing the pressure behind the bullet and cutting its velocity down to the desired level.

Alternatively, specially-manu-factured low-velocity ammunition can be used instead of standard Ball. However, solving the noise problem by decreasing muzzle velocity creates another difficulty: the effective range of the bullet is drastically reduced. Subsonic rifle bullets tend to have a trajectory like a rainbow and an effec-tive range of no more than 218.6yards (290m). The very best sniper-grade subsonic rifle ammunition will allow reasonable accuracy out to about 437.2yards (400m).

Suppressors are also offered for many popular SMGs. Steyr offer a suppressed model of their 9mm AUG, the Chinese make a silenced 7.62mm SMG and the British forces use the L34A1 silenced Sterling.

The Heckler & Koch MP5 SD is a purpose-made suppressed version of the MP5 9mm SMG. This is particular-ly popular with certain specialist units and law enforcement agencies. Even firing short bursts, the sound is not recognizable as a gunshot from more than 164ft (50m) away. The extra weight near the muzzle helps keep the gun on target when firing fully-automatic. For military or police units storming an illegal drugs laboratory, for example, there is another advan-tage: the complete elimination of muzzle blast makes the MP5 SD less liable to ignite the often highly inflam-mable atmosphere found in such buildings.

FOR MANY years grenades were considered to be ultra short-range weapons for the heavy infantryman, with payloads comprising either high-explosive, anti-tank or coloured smoke. The fundamental drawback was that the normal method of projection was throwing, usually by an excited, often tired and always heavily loaded infantryman. As a result they could only be used at very short ranges and were usually relatively inaccurate; not infrequently, they were as dangerous to the thrower or his comrades as to the intended target! Some armies used special devices attached to the muzzle of the standard rifle to project streamlined greandes to somewhat greater ranges, typically 110-330yd (100-300m). In the 1960s, however, modern technology was brought to bear on the subject, as a result of which there has been a great expansion in their use.

Elite forces tend to make more use of grenades than more conventional military units. Indeed, grenades were the primary weapon of the ancestors of modern special warfare units — the elite stormtroop companies of the German Army, created in 1917. They specialized in breaking through enemy positions using infiltration tactics, automatic weapons and a hail of stick grenades.

The most well-known grenade used by Special Forces is the "flash-bang" or "stun" grenade, as used by the British SAS during the storming of the Iranian Embassy in 1980. The whole country watched on live television as the Counter Revolutionary Warfare (CRW) team broke through the doors and windows and vanished inside. The bright flashes and thunderous detonations from within the building told their own story. These devices are widely used by US law enforcement agencies for exact-

Below: US soldier with an M203 grenade launcher fitted to his M16A1 rifle. A single-shot device, M203 launches 40mm grenades over ranges up to 437yd (400m).

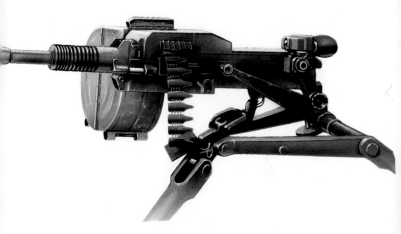

Above: The Soviet AGS-17 is a purpose-built, 30mm automatic grenade launcher. Used by Soviet infantry and special forces, it is also mounted on Mi-8 Hip-E combat assault helicopters.

ly the same purpose: to temporarily incapacitate an armed suspect when police officers storm the building. To soothe liberal political sentiment, they are often referred to as "distraction devices"; this avoids newspaper headlines like: 'Police use grenades to attack suspect's apartment'.

Stun grenades produce a literally blinding flash of light. When they detonate, anyone in the same room is left hopelessly dazzled — as if they had had a powerful camera flash fired straight into their eyes. The grenades also produce a deafening noise: this alone makes people disorientated. The combined effect of the light and noise leaves a terrorist, or other criminal, in no fit state to shoot a weapon as the elite forces troops pour into the room. Stun grenades cause no permanent damage, unless someone's ears are within very close range: in this case, some permanent hearing loss is possible. However, they are very valuable weapons for hostage rescue, helping to save the lives of both hostages and the rescuers.

Elite forces units tasked with anti-terrorist operations also use gas grenades for similar purposes. These are usually filled with CS gas or a similar agent that incapacitates anyone not wearing a respirator. Such chemicals are non-lethal in normal concentrations, although in 1989 Soviet troops killed rioters in Georgia by spraying aerosol cans of gas directly into people's mouths. CS gas grenades have been used in counter-guerrilla operations — US forces used several gases against Viet Cong tunnel complexes during the late 1960s — but they are primarily a weapon for use by dedicated CRW units.

Elite forces soldiers taking part in more conventional operations use the standard types of modern hand grenade. Chunky "pineapple" type grenades of the World War II era have largely been replaced by ones with a thin steel case. Inside is a coil of wire that shatters into a multitude of fragments rather than a handful of iron lumps. They are thus much more likely to wound someone in the target area. Although a grenade's lethal radius is relatively small, on hard ground it can be quite astonishing, and this is reflected in the occasional tragic training accident.

US Army Special Forces were among the first to try out a new type of grenade launcher in Vietnam. During the 1960s, the US Army and Marine Corps issued each rifle squad with one M79 grenade launcher; a single-shot weapon that worked

rather like a break-open shotgun. This was a very useful weapon, offering infantry units their own "mini-howitzer", but a soldier carrying an M79 could not carry a rifle as well. Then came the XM148, which fired the same 40mm grenade, but fitted underneath the barrel of an M16 rifle. Special Forces patrols reported favorably. It was equally useful for pinning down an enemy unit and allowing US troops to maneuver around their flank. For a small patrol, trying to break contact with a larger enemy formation, it was a valuable source of extra firepower. The idea was developed by the AAI Corporation, and the resulting M203 40mm grenade launcher replaced the M79. British special forces have used both types of grenade launcher both in Northern Ireland and the Falkland Islands.

The M203 fires a 40mm grenade to

Above: FFV 915 smoke grenade on a Swedish AK4 7.62mm rifle. It can be fired from any rifle fitted with the standard 22mm grenade launcher.

a maximum effective range of 1,312ft (400m). A single-shot breechloader, it weighs 3.1lb (1.4kg) and fires HE, smoke or illuminating rounds.

The US Navy SEAL teams that raided the coastline of occupied Kuwait in February 1991, used a rather heavier weapon. The Mk19 40mm grenade launcher is a belt-fed machine gun that was developed for the Navy in 1966. Fitted to the PBRs and other river craft used by the "Brown Water" fleet in Vietnam, it remains in widespread use aboard light vessels like the SEALs' speedboats.

The Mk19 is an air-cooled blowback machine gun with a cyclic rate of fire

Above: The Soviet AGS-17 automatic grenade launcher nicknamed Plamya (Flame). It has an effective range of 875-1,312yd (800-1,200m). The drum magazine contains a total of 30-rounds.

Left: Haley & Weller E182 multiburst stun grenades use the H&W patented silent electrical ignition system; the lever does not leave the grenade, nor is there any discernable sound of a cap firing.

of 375 rounds per minute. Fed from a 20- or 50-round distintegrating link belt, it fires from the open bolt position and has an effective range of approximately 5,250ft (1,600m). Ammunition includes HE, armor-piercing and dual-purpose armor-piercing grenades.

Soviet Spetsnaz special forces have similar weapons to their US counterparts. There is an underbarrel 30mm grenade launcher similar to the M203 fitted to AK-74 assault rifles. The Soviet equivalent to the Mk19 is the AGS-17; a tripod-mounted 30mm grenade launcher that proved so successful in Afghanistan that every Soviet infantry company was issued with a pair of them. Fitted to Mi-8 helicopters and to armored personnel carriers, it provided the high-angle fire so necessary in mountain warfare.

EVER since the widespread use of specialist military units during World War II, all manner of exotic weapons and equipment have been developed for their use. The rapid expansion of US Special Forces during the Vietnam War led to renewed interest in specialist equipment. Many other armies have found themselves involved in conflicts for which special forces are ideally suited — and have produced unusual equipment specifically for their elite units.

Amphibious warfare equipment

The US elite forces still lead the world in the range and quality of special-purpose military equipment. Of the various elite US formations, the US Navy SEALs have probably the greatest range of exotic kit. They are trained to undertake a breathtaking variety of missions, and their amphibious role demands some very specialized equipment indeed.

SEAL combat swimmers do not use normal Self-Contained Underwater Breathing Apparatus (SCUBA) gear. The sort of open-circuit systems familiar to civilian divers leave a telltale trail of bubbles. In calm water, this would allow a sharp-eyed enemy soldier to pinpoint a diver when he is

at his most vulnerable. For beach reconnaissance or sabotage missions against harbors, the SEALs employ the Draeger LAR-V closed circuit pure oxygen system. However, pure oxygen can only be used at shallow depths: at greater pressure it is necessary to use a gas/air mix. SEAL teams of both the Atlantic and Pacific Fleets also use the Carleton Technologies Closed circuit Oxygen Breathing Apparatus (COBRA), which can be mounted on the diver's chest or back. Costing up to $30,000 each, COBRA units provide three to four hour's of oxygen.

In the warm waters of the Persian Gulf, hypothermia is not a major problem for amphibious troops. However, Iran and Iraq have both used chemical weapons and contaminated water is a serious hazard for combat swimmers. So too is the cold in more northerly waters. To protect themselves in both cases, the SEALs are equipped with dry suits: worn over uniform, these waterproof rubber garments rely on the trapped air layer to insulate the diver from the cold. They can cost over $2,500 each and incorporate numerous special features. For example, divers trying to neutralize enemy mines underwater have to have non-

Above: As terrorists become more sophisticated special forces have started to use helmets with all-round head and neck protection.

Left: Special forces have led development of the humble bayonet into a multi-purpose tool. This Soviet bayonet is also a saw and a wire-cutter.

magnetic air valves. Swimming in close proximity to a magnetic-influence mine could be unnecessarily risky for a diver in standard kit.

Although their individual equipment is often the most expensive in the US forces, not all SEAL gear is the product of ultra-modern technology. During Operation *Desert Storm*, the SEALs operating in the Persian Gulf signalled their headquarters in California to send them 50 "boogie boards". A Navy officer bought them in a surf shop and had the small surf boards flown out: the SEALs needed them to help swim long distances in shallow Gulf waters.

Mini-submarines

Combat swimmers do not rely solely on swimming for clandestine underwater operations. The SEALs also go to war in SEAL Delivery Vehicles (SDVs): mini-submarines that can be launched from warships. Several nuclear-powered ballistic missile submarines have been converted to carry SDVs; the SEALs can board the SDVs from inside the submarine and launch them without breaking surface.

Other navies have similar systems — the Soviets have modified several of their submarines and it was interesting to note the appearance of several Royal Navy submarines coming back from the Gulf War. Several Oberon class diesel-electric submarines returned to port with typical panache, flying the "Jolly Roger" with a cloak and dagger emblem attached — the RN submariners' traditional sign that they have been engaged on covert inshore operations. The submarines were painted in a spectacular disruptive camouflage scheme used to good effect when in clear, shallow waters.

Raiding craft

Amphibious specialists like the SEALs also require specialist surface craft: the SEALs use Zodiac F-470 inflatable rubber boats. Some 13.6ft (4.14m) long, they weigh 260lb (118kg) and can be inflated in only 90 seconds. Fitted with outboard motors capable of delivering between 25 and 50hp, they can accommodate a seven-man SEAL squad and all its equipment. The British SBS uses similar kit.

Elite forces equipment can often be disguised or given dual roles — and this is particularly true of small warships. For instance, the Royal Navy's Archer class boats — publicly tasked with Search-and-Rescue — are also designed to carry boats for the SBS. The US Navy operates a number of light craft for the same purpose, including the Uniflite Sea Fox fiberglass craft designed for high-speed dashes into enemy waters. The Peterson Builders patrol boat is a vessel capable of over 30 knots and is fitted with cannon, grenade launchers and machine-guns. In December 1991, the US Navy commissioned the first of a new class of Patrol Boat, Coastal (ABC). Over 164ft (50m) long, the PBCs have a range of over 2,000 nautical miles and will travel at 35 knots carrying two complete SEAL squads and their Zodiac boats.

Parachute techniques

The SEALs, the British SAS and SBS and other special warfare units are also trained to enter the combat zone from the air. For many years, the well-known technique referred to as High-Altitude Low-Opening (HALO) was employed: jumping from altitudes of over 25,000 feet (7,625m), soldiers used a free-fall descent until the last moment. Usually conducted at night, the aim was to disguise the Drop Zone from inquisitive eyes and radar systems. Today, special forces personnel are equally likely to employ High-Altitude High-Opening (HAHO) techniques. Using their steerable parachutes and, in the case of US troops, global positioning receivers for precise navigation, they can leap from their aircraft when up to 31.2 miles (50km) away from their pre-selected Drop Zone.

Body armor

Elite forces units tasked with counter-terrorist operations are used to using body armor. For hostage rescue missions, such as the famous SAS assault on the Iranian Embassy, it is essential. Because body armor has been worn by many law enforcement officers in the USA, there is a great deal of data available, demonstrating its critical value. Over the last 10 years or so, it has saved between 400 and 450 police lives in the USA alone.

A military unit's choice of body armor depends on the anticipated threat. Bullets' powers of penetration depend on their weight, velocity, shape and construction. The sort of weapons typically encountered by US police officers — "Saturday night specials" in .25in or .380in Auto caliber — can be stopped by a relatively thin Kevlar vest worn underneath normal clothing or uniform. Elite forces soldiers often require a higher level of protection to face more powerful pistol, SMG and rifle bullets.

Above: SEALs rehearse a diving drill from a Zodiac F-470.

Below: The F-470 inflatable can carry up to seven men equipped.

There is an inevitable weight penalty. To protect a soldier's back and chest from 7.62mm ammunition can add another 22lb (10kg) to an already over-burdened man. One option, offered by several manufacturers, is to use a special insert that will keep out high-velocity rifle rounds in a vest that is otherwise proof against pistol ammunition. In counter-terrorist action, armor can sometimes be very closely tailored to the circumstances. For

Below: Dressed for operations a special forces soldier wears modern body armor, both more effective and easier to wear than that in use ten years ago.

instance, exercises have shown that the first two men in an entry team can get inside the target building before the terrorists have time to react. By the time they bring their guns to bear, the third man is on his way in. In some siege situations, the third man in the team has worn much heavier armor for just this reason.

In the Iranian Embassy and many other shoot-outs between terrorists and army elite forces, the soldiers had armor and their enemies did not. However, access to body armor is becoming more common, and soldiers cannot rely on always enjoying such an advantage. Although terrorists have not made a Lod

Airport-style suicide raid for some years, the prospect of yet another kamikaze mission by a terrorist gang in body armor is a nightmarish possibility. As a result, several armies are experimenting with armor-piercing ammunition. The US Joint Services Small Arms Program is evaluating a 9mm armor-piercing bullet developed by Swedish Ordnance. This combines a steel jacket with a lead core and will penetrate 65-70 layers of Kevlar. The company's tungsten-cored 5.56mm rifle ammunition is also under test.

In the UK, FR Ordnance International has developed a cut-down version of the H&K G3 rifle that is not significantly bigger than an MP5 SMG. The MC51 fires 7.62mm x 51 NATO bullets at 2,128.7ft/s (649m/s) and has four times the muzzle energy of a 9mm 2Z fired from a typical sub-machine gun. It will pass clean through concealed soft body armor. Firing armor-piercing rounds, it will penetrate 0.5in (12.7mm) of steel at close range.

Sighting equipment

Elite forces units can afford to use the latest technical innovations from the shooting industry. Over the last few years, many companies have developed new optical sights for sports shooting, hunting — and military use. These range from simple schemes such as tritium inserts on standard iron sights: they are visible in the dark rather like a luminous watch dial.

Rather more complex are the numerous "red dot" scopes produced for handguns and rifles. These first appeared during the late 1960s but have only recently achieved commercial success. For handguns or SMGs, they have no magnification. The shooter keeps both eyes open and focuses on a single red dot within the sight — the dot shows where the bullet will strike and it does not have to be centred. Sight acquisition is very quick and it is ideal for rapid shooting at close ranges, particularly in poor light conditions.

"Red dot" scopes such as the Aimpoint or Ultradot should not be confused with laser sights that actually project a thin beam of light onto the target. Beloved by film directors, the laser sights illuminate the point of impact — a highly disagreeable prospect for the intended target!

All these systems have their disadvantages. They are more suitable for counter-terrorist operations rather than extended service under field conditions. Laser sights are of limited value in bright sunshine and do not work as well against very dark colors

Below: Special forces soldiers must be ready to fight in any environment at any time. This Canadian Special Service Force soldier has snow overclothes.

that tend to absorb the red dot rather than reflect it.

Heavy weapons

Most special forces units tend to operate in small patrols, tasked with reconnaissance or small-scale raids behind enemy lines. However, there are occasions when heavy weapons such as anti-tank rockets are essential. The US Army has recently adopted the AT-4 shoulder-fired rocket as its lightest infantry anti-tank system. A modernized version of the Swedish Carl Gustav weapon only just being replaced in the British

Below: This all-purpose knife and carrying case is the type of equipment that can be found in the kit of British special forces troopers.

Below: An engineer of the US Army's SOF prepares to blow a demolition charge using an electrical detonator. His weapon is an Israeli 9mm UZI SMG.

FN range of protective vests

Armor thickness	Weapon type	Calibers	Distance	Vest weight
0.08in (2mm	Pistol	0.22in; 7.65mm 0.38in; .45in; 9mm	9.8ft (3m)	7.9lb (3.6kg)
0.12in (3mm)	Pistol	0.22in; 7.65mm; 7.62mm Tokarev; 0.38in; .45in; 9mm	9.8ft (3m)	11.5lb (5.2kg)
	SMG	0.45in; 9mm		
	Carbine	0.30in	82ft (25m)	
0.16in (4mm)	Rifle	7.62mm Kalashnikov	16.8ft (5m)	15lb (6.8kg)
0.26in (6.5mm)	Rifle	7.62mm NATO 5.56mm NATO	16.8ft (5m)	24lb (10.9kg)

Above: Despite extra clothing and equipment SF soldiers must be able to undertake hazardous physical tasks and still be ready to fire their weapons at any time.

Army, the AT-4 takes the place of the elderly Light Anti-Tank Weapon (LAW). The LAW was used in Vietnam as a "bunker buster"; this light, one-shot rocket was used for the same purpose during the Falklands conflict. US Special Forces in the Gulf complained that the AT-4, while much better at its primary role — knocking out tanks — is too heavy. Special Forces patrols were not engaging armor.

The US Marine Corps recognized this problem first. Since they spent much of World War II assaulting elaborate defensive systems on Pacific islands, the Marines have always maintained an interest in specialist assault weapons. The Marines are currently equipped with several "bunker busters". The Brunswick Rifleman's Assault Weapon is a 5.5in (140mm) diameter sphere, containing a choice of HE, hollow charge, smoke or incendiary payloads. Fired from an attachment fitted to an M16 rifle, it has an effective range of 656ft (200m).

The Marines also employ a bazooka-type system called the Shoulder-launched Multi-purpose Assault Weapon (SMAW), that proved so successful during the Gulf War that neighbouring US Army units borrowed them. SMAW looks like an anti-tank rocket, but its 13.5lb (6.1kg) warhead is designed to penetrate steel reinforced concrete bunkers or substantial earthworks.

ALL TYPES of warfare have developed their own 'electronic battlefields' over the past 30 years and no element of the armed forces have been keener to use such modern technology to support their activities than the special forces. This especially applies in the area of sensors where electronics, optics and other more esoteric technologies can be used to detect enemies, to ascertain where they are, in what strength, how they are armed and equipped, and how they are behaving.

The popular image of elite forces soldiers tends to be along the lines of the heavily-armed Action Man constantly on the attack — the reality is very different. Many elite forces soldiers are reconnaissance specialists, trained to operate behind enemy lines. They do not rush about the battlefield: on the contrary, they have to be able to stay out of sight by day and night, lying-up in a cramped dugout. A four-man team, studying enemy activities from their underground Observation Post (OP) rely on the most up-to-date sensors to gather intelligence. Thermal imagers and infra-red scopes provide visual assistance while seismic detectors and ground radar systems cover areas the team cannot see. Information can be reported back using burst transmission satellite-linked radios.

The British Army has employed much the same techniques and equipment whether training "stay behind" parties for the anticipated Warsaw Pact invasion, or when monitoring terrorist activity in Northern Ireland. Close Observation Platoons tend to attract the most dedicated soldiers: men who have the patience to lie in a concealed dug-out for days on end. There can be no cooking, in case the smell betrays their presence, and all personal administration must take place in the same cramped space. Wrapping your excrement in cling film and tucking it in the rubbish bag is a far cry from *Rambo* movies!

The full range of sensors currently in service is classified. Since they are constantly in service against terrorists, their exact capabilities must remain a closely-guarded secret. Nevertheless, the basic systems are well understood. The British Army has used several kinds. IRIS is an infra-red beam that signals its control when a passing man or vehicle interrupts it. This, and similar infra-red beam systems are usually set some distance above the ground — otherwise animals on the move during the night will constantly trigger them off. Another old British system, TOBIAS, relies on geophones to detect sound waves transmitted through the earth by footfalls or vehicle movement.

Covert Local Area Sensor System for Intruder Classification (CLASSIC) is a modern electronic monitoring machine manufactured by Racal. Each CLASSIC system consists of a monitor and up to eight remote sensors. The latter have either geophones

Below: Devices like this Barr & Stroud Thermal Imager are essential for surveillance. The passive IR18 sees through mist, smoke and shadow.

Above: Rigid borescopes can be used to observe through apparently solid objects. Direct viewing is possible; or cameras can be attached.

or infra-red detectors and relay their information to the monitor. Pressure pad switches and trip wires can also be attached to the system. A typical scenario for which CLASSIC is used might involve the covert observation of a minor road bridge. The patrol discovers a good location from which the target area can be observed, but from which their own position can be approached by a hidden route that would keep the enemy out of sight until they were practically on top of the OP. Using CLASSIC, the patrol could rely on the sensors to alert them to any activity behind them.

The performance of seismic detectors depends heavily on the type of ground on which they are used. In good conditions they can pick up the footsteps of an individual person at up to several thousand metres, but soft ground, rain and other distractions can reduce this figure substantially. The US Army's AN/TRS-2(V) Platoon Early Warning System has an effective range of 4,920ft (1,500m).

Elite forces patrols also employ ground radar devices. The US Army's Model 386 lightweight ground surveillance radar, manufactured by General Dynamics, is typical of the systems suitable for infantry patrols.

This tripod-mounted X-band radar provides 360° coverage to a maximum range of 19,680ft (6,000m).

Visual surveillance devices have improved considerably over the last ten years. Older equipment, like the British Army's Individual Weapon Sight (IWS) provided a reasonable image in the right conditions, but tended to be heavy and tiring to use. After 20 minutes or so staring at a target through the IWS, a soldier's eyes become very tired. Observation duty must be rotated every half-hour at the least. The latest passive night goggles work on the same principle, but provide a better picture and are less likely to give the operator a headache. However, all Image Intensifiers rely on available light, amplifying it about 100,000 times: their performance is reduced by rain, snow, smoke or fog.

Thermal imagers are far better: but at £25,000 each, they should be. Providing a good picture through smoke and fog as well as the darkest night, they allow the skilled operator to distinguish between types of vehicle — although it must be noted that vehicle recognition through a thermal imager is much harder than with binoculars during daylight. Because they pick up heat sources, an image of a tank tends to emphasize the vehicle's hottest areas — its engine, tracks and barrel. Telling the difference between types of Soviet main battle tank using only a thermal imager demands a high standard of training.

SPECIAL forces have unique communications requirements due to their special roles and the command links that are associated with them. Many special operations, such as the release of hostages, are politically extremely delicate and as a result they are directed in some detail from the very highest government levels. This creates something of a communications problem within the national territory, but is even more difficult when the force is deployed into a foreign country at some distance from its homeland, such as, for example, the West German GSG-9 at Mogadishu and the US Delta Force on the Iranian operation to rescue the Embassy hostages.

Strategic communications must be secure, rapid and reliable to provide two-way communications between the deployed force commander and the political minister responsible for the direction of the operation, who will usually be located in a specially equipped crisis-management center. The latter requires regular, accurate and timely updating on events on the ground so that, in combination with other inputs, decisions can be made with confidence and quickly promulgated.

Within the deployed force there is a requirement for rapid communications down to the lowest level, in many cases not just to team leaders, but also to every individual soldier. These radios should, if possible, be secure, since many modern terrorists have a monitoring capabilty. However, modern techniques enable this to be achieved without too much difficulty. The old-fashioned 'scambler' has long been overtaken by much more effective modern means of on-line electronic encryption. For example, in a voice radio a pseudo-random pulse train, controlled by an operator-inserted key-setting, can be added to the digitised voice signal to encrypt it, with the reverse process taking place at the receiving set to convert the signal back to comprehensible speech.

For special forces at some distance from their base long-range ground- or sky-wave sets still have considerable importance, and the British MEL UK/PRC-319 is achieving considerable success in this field. This is an HF/VHF tactical radio covering the frequency band 1.5-40MHz. Very light in weight for the facilities it provides it is easily manpacked, comprising four units: a transmitter/receiver unit;

Below: The sheer compactness of today's lap-top computers and communications systems has proved to be of great benefit when in the field.

Above: The revolutionary British PRC-319 radio combines great range with highly sophisticated modes of operation, including burst transmission. It is in wide SF service.

an electronic message unit (EMU); and two antenna tuners. It operates using one frequency for transmit and a separate frequency for receive, and to enhance resistance to detection does not use an intermediate frequency (IF) internally. The EMU is an alphanumeric device with built-in cyrpto and has a 2,000 character memory. The PRC-319 employs 'burst transmission', which means that the message to be sent is prepared by typing it into the EMU where it is electronically encrypted; then, on the operator's instruction it is sent in a very short period of time. Thus, a message which could take several minutes to send by voice or teleprinter can be sent in less than 10 seconds. This technique makes it virtually impossible for hostile forces to detect, record, jam or direction-find (DF) the transmission.

The security forces also need to listen into the terrorists and to detect any electronic devices they may be using. This requires sophisticated monitoring equipment covering as broad a segment of the electromagnetic frequency band as possible. Such equipment is essentially similar to the 'detector vans' used to discover unlicensed domestic TV receivers in the United Kingdom. It can pinpoint the location of target devices operated by illegal organisations quickly, reliably and with considerable accuracy.

The security forces can also use electronic devices to disrupt terrorist communications by jamming. This is ideally done using 'spot' jamming on a specific frequency, since this can be done with great accuracy and thus not disrupt other communications systems that are using adjacent frequencies.

There is a host of modern jammers available, ranging from large, multi-capable devices to very small unattended, expendable jammers, which can be placed by hand near to the target transmitter, especially in anti-terrorist operations. A typical expendable device (Racal RJS3140) weighs 2.5kg (including batteries), has an operating life of at least 120 minutes minutes, can be set to any frequency in the band 20-90MHz, to cover a bandwidth selectable between 1 and 31MHz, and can be programmed to switch on at a specified time. Such a device would be ideal for use in jamming terrorist communications in the period immediately prior to an attack. However, few terrorists are so unsophisticated in this increasingly electronic age as to stick to one frequency and may even soon use frequency-hopping sets. Such sets are best attacked using a wide-band jammer ideally positioned very close by to the enemy radio.

During Operation *Desert Storm*, British and US special forces inside Kuwait and Iraq used several types of Fast Attack Vehicle (FAV), sometimes erroneously described as a "dune buggy". These adaptions of off-road racing cars look more at home in a *Mad Max* movie than a modern army, but they are tremendously useful machines. Bristling with communications and navigational gear, with machine guns fitted and substantial roll-bars to protect the occupants from the almost inevitable crashes, these bizarre vehicles proved very successful. Able to drive cross country at up to 60mph (96.5km/h), the FAVs can traverse sand berms over two metres in height.

The US Navy SEALs drive FAVs manufactured by Chenowth Racing Products. Their preferred armament is a pair of 7.62mm M60 machine guns, one at the front and one at the rear. Costing $50,000 each, these were the first Coalition vehicles to enter Kuwait City.

There are few other vehicles specifically manufactured for special forces use. The majority of vehicles employed by specialist units are simply conversions of existing military equipment. For examle, the British

SAS have been using their famous "Pink Panther" Land Rovers for over 20 years. These are heavily-modified military Land Rovers, designed for long-range patrolling in the desert. Used in counter-insurgency campaigns in Oman and other parts of the Middle East, they can carry a tremendous variety of weapons. In the open desert, long range weapons are essential: "Pink Panthers" can swap their 7.62mm GPMGs for Browning M2 .50in caliber machine guns, 20mm cannon, or MILAN anti-tank missiles. Cannon and machine guns are normally fitted with spent cartridge bins to collect the empty brass. Firing on the move without one tends to shower the occupants with bullet cases: a hazard to crew and vehicle alike.

The new Land Rover 110 series, as modified for elite forces' use, incorporates many extra features. Two banks of smoke dischargers fitted to the front bumper can create an instant smoke screen in front of the Rover if a hasty withdrawal is necessary. The

Below: A pair of Emerson Fast Attack Vehicles used by US Special Forces. Such vehicles are both rugged and versatile.

Above: Synonymous with covert operations by the SAS for decades, the Land Rover can fulfil many operational roles.

Rover carries a winch and towing cable to pull itself, or other vehicles out of trouble. A spring suspension system, copied from the Range Rover, gives an unprecendentedly comfortable ride over rough terrain. The vehicle has extra fuel tanks under both front seats and in the rear. The windshield is normally removed and the vehicles can be fitted with armor plate if desired.

The Land Rover 110 gearbox has two gear ranges, offering 10 forward gears. It has excellent control in low-range, four-wheel drive engaging automatically. High-range is used for normal driving on roads and a separate knob must be used to engage four-wheel drive, since this is not normally required. Using four-wheel drive on roads causes increased tyre wear.

The collapse of the Warsaw Pact removed one of the most interesting collections of special forces vehicles from the world stage. Until 1989, the East German Army maintained several companies of armored troops equipped with American M48 tanks and M113 armored personnel carriers acquired from Vietnam. Painted in West German markings, they were trained to pass through the frontline to create havoc in NATO rear areas.

Below: Dirt bikes provide a high degree of mobility.

OTHER SUPER-VALUE MILITARY GUIDES IN THIS SERIES

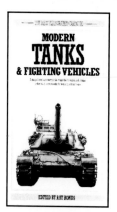

THE NEW ILLUSTRATED GUIDE TO

MODERN
TANKS
& FIGHTING VEHICLES

EDITED BY RAY BONDS

THE NEW ILLUSTRATED GUIDE TO

MODERN
RIFLES
& SUB-MACHINE GUNS

The most formidable weapons of this modern era

MAJOR FREDERICK MYATT M.C.

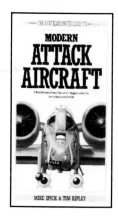

THE NEW ILLUSTRATED GUIDE TO

MODERN
ATTACK
AIRCRAFT

MIKE SPICK & TIM RIPLEY

THE NEW ILLUSTRATED GUIDE TO

MODERN
ELITE
FORCES

MAX WALMER

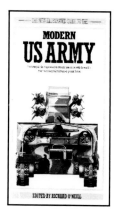

THE NEW ILLUSTRATED GUIDE TO

MODERN
US ARMY

EDITED BY RICHARD O'NEILL

THE NEW ILLUSTRATED GUIDE TO

MODERN
SUB
HUNTERS

DAVID MILLER

OTHER ILLUSTRATED MILITARY GUIDES AVAILABLE

Modern US Fighters and Attack Aircraft
Modern US Navy
Modern Warships
Aircraft Markings
Allied Fighters of World War II

★ Each title has 160 fact-filled pages
★ Each is colorfully illustrated with hundreds of action photographs and technical drawings
★ Each contains concisely presented data and accurate descriptions of major international weapons systems
★ Each title represents tremendous value for money